THE
COTTAGE BOOK

THE
COTTAGE BOOK
The Undiscovered Country Diary
of an Edwardian Statesman

By Sir Edward and Lady Grey

Edited and Introduced
by Michael Waterhouse

VICTOR GOLLANCZ

LONDON

Acknowlededgments

I am most grateful to English Country Cottages of Earby, Lancashire, for their support and assistance in connection with the publication of *The Cottage Book*.

I would particularly like to thank Sir Edward Grey's great nephew, Mr Christopher Graves, for his agreement to publish the *Cottage Book*. He specifically asked that I make charitable donations to the North Atlantic Salmon Fund and the Edward Grey Institute of Field Ornithology at Oxford University. In addition I am most grateful for his kindness and encouragement throughout the period of my research.

I would also like to thank Lady Alethea Eliot for her permission to publish her father's, Sidney Buxton's, tribute to Edward Grey. She has kindly given her original copy of the *Cottage Book* to the current owners of Fallodon Hall, Mr and Mrs Peter Bridgeman.

Finally I would like to thank Mrs Rhoda Batty and the Hampshire County Library for the provision of prints from Heywood Sumner's book *The Itchen Valley* (1881), and Mr Edward Roberts of Cheriton who supplied the local photographs.

A CIP catalogue record for this book is available from the British Library
ISBN 0 297 82534 8

Designed by Peter Butler
Typeset in Garamond
Printed and bound in Italy

Gollancz
The Orion Publishing Group
5 Upper St Martin's Lane
London
WC2H 9EA

CONTENTS

Dedicated to the memory of Sir Edward and Lady Grey,
Northumbrians with Hampshire written in their hearts.

He does not die that can bequeath
Some influence to the land he knows,
Or dares, persistent, interwreath
Love permanent with the wild hedgerows;

The spring's superb adventure calls
His dust athwart the woods to flame;
His boundary river's secret falls
Perpetuate and repeat his name.
He rides his loud October sky;
He does not die, he does not die.

HILLAIRE BELLOC

For Lucinda, Robin and Marcus

In the following lines Dorothy Grey once tried to express
what the Cottage life meant to her; lines left imperfect
and never finished, but which still show her feeling:*

Dear Itchen country, kind through all the year,
Soft winter brightness and full summer green.
Light-soiled and joyful, and all the seasons seem
Specially meaning and full-hearted here.
The water meadows lying in a cool dusk
Stretch westward to the arch of evening light.
The soft mist rises, rolled in lines of white,
Wrapping the river in its yellow musk.
Dear Cottage, with its happiness and peace
And quiet breathing leisure, sweetly spent
Far from all uglyness and tiresome show,
A place for watching nature's still increase,
A refuge from all hurt till life shall end,
A nest where love and wisdom still may grow.

* SOURCE: *Memoir of Dorothy Grey* by Mrs Mandell Creighton.

The author and publishers remind readers that the land surrounding Sir Edward Grey's cottage is private property, and that the rights of the owner must be respected.

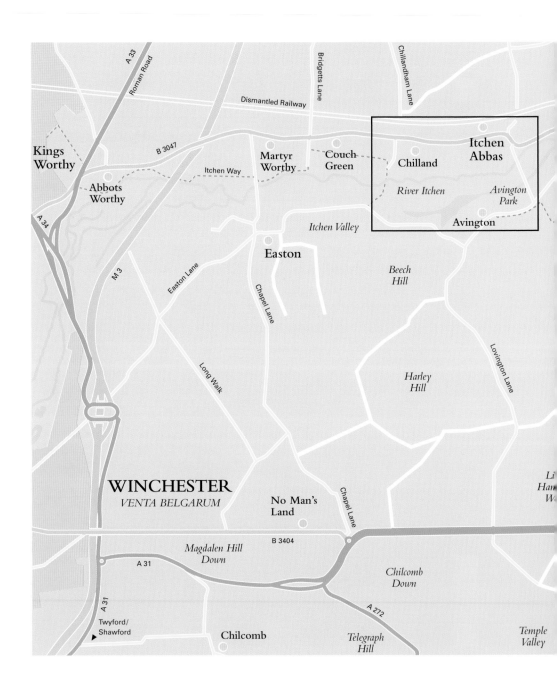

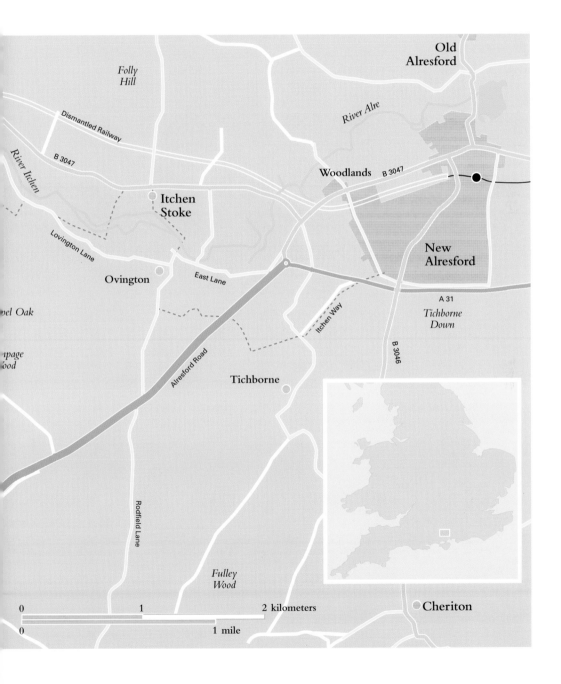

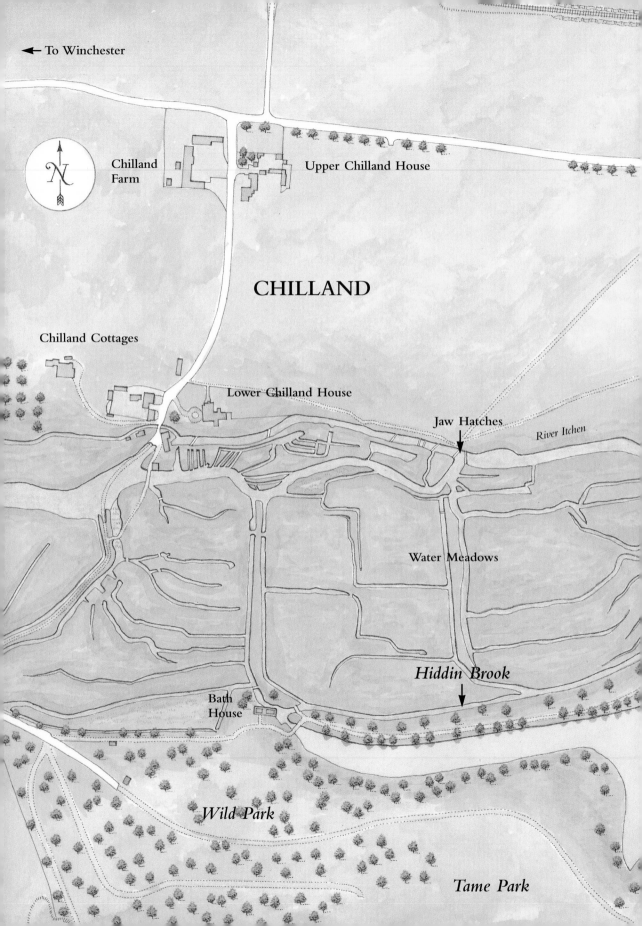

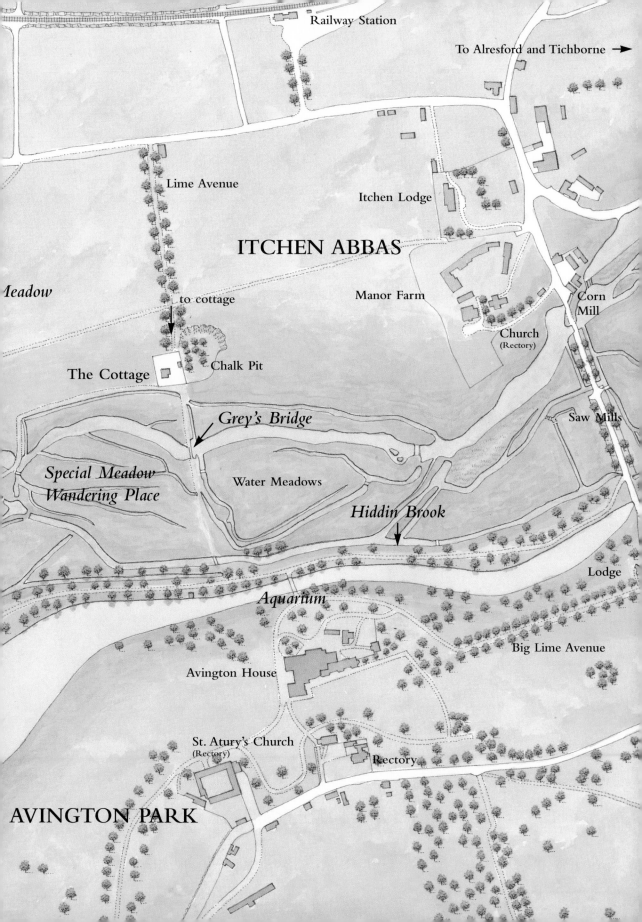

INTRODUCTION

I

Sir Edward Grey played a vitally important role on the diplomatic stage at the beginning of the twentieth century. He struggled desperately to preserve the peace during the run-up to the First World War. Yet he only went abroad once during his eleven-year tenure at the Foreign Office. Most weekends, unable to make the long journey to his family seat at Fallodon in Northumberland, he took the train from Waterloo to the little Hampshire village of Itchen Abbas, near Winchester. Here, with his wife Dorothy, he would fish on the river and enjoy a reclusive love affair with nature, immortalized in later years in his books.

Many people have kept journals on the flora and fauna around their idyllic country retreat. What is it then that is so captivating about the *Cottage Book*? My own fascination with it began around one hundred years after Grey compiled the *Cottage Book*, when I started to keep a diary about the birdlife surrounding my own weekend cottage on the edge of the Cotswolds. Sometimes we would stay in Hampshire with my wife's family who lived a few miles from Itchen Abbas, just below the downs. I had ample opportunity to retrace the Greys' footsteps and to rediscover their 'places' as well as their birds.

Sir Edward Grey in 1894 as Parliamentary Under-Secretary at the Foreign Office

Dorothy Grey in 1890

The *Cottage Book* begins in March 1894. Gladstone had finally retired and Lord Rosebery became Prime Minister. Grey was undertaking his first ministerial brief, as 'number two' at the Foreign Office to Lord Kimberley. He wrote in his autobiography:

It began from a desire to leave on Monday something which would tell us what to look for on the following Saturday, and the first entries were written solely for this purpose. But it became much more than that. It was a record of our stay there and of our feelings and enjoyment. It was always left open so that either of us might write in it when we felt moved to do so. The entries made by my wife are marked with the 'D'; my own are similarly marked with the letter 'E'.

They both continued to add entries throughout a decade of Liberal opposition until Dorothy's untimely death and Grey's appointment as Foreign Secretary late in 1905. He had the *Cottage Book* privately published in very small numbers in 1909.

Sir Edward said one had to be happy to write a book. He produced two classic books on his major interests outside politics – *Fly Fishing* (1899) and *The Charm of Birds* (1927). The former was written when he was married to Dorothy and, a quarter of a century later, he drew on his memories of the Itchen valley to produce *The Charm of Birds*, surely one of the finest books ever written on birdsong. The *Cottage Book* provided the groundwork for it. Grey's second marriage – to long-time friend Pamela Glenconner – coincided with the writing of his autobiography, *Twenty-Five Years*, and a collection of lectures given between 1919 and 1924, published as *The Fallodon Papers*.

By his early thirties Grey had become an ornithologist of considerable skill. Anyone who can identify the song of the lesser whitethroat (see the May 15 1896 entry) is no beginner, although this knowledge had not been with him as a young man. He admits in *The Charm of Birds*:

> I arrived at the age of manhood knowing only the songs of two individual birds; one was a robin, whose tameness and persistence in singing when there is hardly further song to be heard forces anyone to know its voice. Then there were thrushes and blackbirds between which I could not distinguish, and for the purpose of song represented to me one species.

It was undoubtedly Dorothy who gave Grey the interest in birds that became such an important part of his life. There is evidence for this in a charming entry in the *Cottage Book* for May 22 1902:

> I hardly dare write anything about birds; I am so overshadowed by D. I went with her on Tuesday to be shown the stone curlew's eggs—we spied and stalked and crept and saw a stone curlew standing by a ragged lonely whin bush on the down, like a sentinel. As we got nearer, it trotted off with the step of a ghost in the evening light passed the nest and disappeared.

We should not be surprised if Grey comes across as a countryman rather than a politician in the *Cottage Book* as he spent his formative years at his family home deep in rural Northumberland. Fallodon is a 2000-acre estate that sits between the Cheviot Hills and the bleak, romantic Northumbrian coast near

Alnwick. It was in the burns of Fallodon that he learnt to fish for brown trout and on the neighbouring moors that he grew to love the wild, evocative call of the curlew. In 1884, after being sent down from Oxford, Grey started his wildlife sanctuary at Fallodon. It consisted of two ponds surrounded by a fox-proof fence. He bred many different species of duck that were always kept unpinioned, and a list of the ducks that bred was kept in the *Fallodon Green Book*, which started in 1888 and stretched to beyond Dorothy's death in 1906. Like his fellow Northumbrian, St Cuthbert, Grey had an amazing ability to tame birds and wild animals. At meal times shovellers would feed at his feet, teal from his hand, and mandarin ducks and robins would alight on his head.

As his father died young, Grey and his five brothers and sisters were brought up by their grandfather, Sir George Grey, a former Home Secretary. Edward was given a traditional education at Winchester – where he developed two passions that stayed with him for the rest of his life: the art of dry-fly fishing and a love of the River Itchen. He failed academically at Oxford, and was rusticated in 1884, but he went back to take a third in Jurisprudence and, ironically, over forty years later, he became Chancellor of the university.

From Oxford he went north to Fallodon. His grandfather had died two years before and Grey assumed responsibility for the running of the family estate as well as commencing his long career as a public servant. By the close of 1885 Grey had become both a married man and the newly elected Liberal MP for Berwick-upon-Tweed.

Dorothy Widdrington was a withdrawn, shy and intelligent girl who, in the words of George Macaulay Trevelyan, 'was more in harmony with nature than any human being'. Their close and happy marriage was based on common tastes and interests: the country, books and poetry, especially Wordsworth. In 1892 Gladstone made Grey Under-Secretary of State for Foreign Affairs. Grey was a minister for only one year during the period covered by the *Cottage Book*. In June 1895 Lord Rosebery's Government was defeated in a division on the War Office vote in the House and resigned. The Liberals were then in opposition for a decade. His three-year period in office was relatively uneventful, with one exception alluded to in a *Cottage Book* entry for March 31 1895: 'Pruning Sunday. Disturbed by work and have to go up on Sunday evening.' 'Grey's Declaration', as it became known, resulted from a rumoured French expedition from West Africa across the continent to the headwaters of the Nile into the Sudan – a territory over which Britain's

The rose-covered front of the cottage facing the river. Note the corrugated iron roof, the lime avenue behind and the small lawn where the Grey's would sleep out on a summer's night.

claims were well known. Grey informed the Commons in no uncertain terms that such action would be considered unfriendly. The speech proved very useful a few years later when Kitchener had taken Khartoum and came across the Marchand expedition being conducted under the French flag. This became known as the 'Fashoda Incident'.

The stresses of office sharpened the pleasures of weekends at the cottage. The personal significance of both the place and the diary are described by Grey in his autobiography:

Dorothy sitting in the cottage doorway. Looking from 'Grey's Bridge', this must have been taken just after the cottage was erected in 1890 as there are no climbers growing up the trellis.

We intended it only as a fishing cottage, but it became much more and we made a special life there. It was to both of us a lovely refuge. I refused ever to make a political speech within miles of it. We spent every weekend there, refusing invitations which might interfere with it. What the life was may be understood from a little diary called *Cottage Book*, which I had privately printed after my wife's death... We rented a house in Grosvenor Road, and when we were in Office from 1892 to 1894, and unable to get away from London until the Saturday morning, we used to call ourselves by an alarm clock and walk over Lambeth Bridge...up to Waterloo Station and down by the 6 o'clock train to Itchen Abbas Station, whence it was but a few steps to the old lime avenue which led down to our cottage. Trout fishing in that part of the river was excellent... I still kept my old habit of not fishing on Sunday, but spending it by bicycling about the country, and revisiting particular spots that had some particular merit at a certain time of the year. In this way the cottage at Itchen became to us even dearer than Fallodon itself. It was something special and sacred, outside the ordinary stream of life.

Mrs Mandell Creighton* published a private memoir of Dorothy in 1907, in which she evoked the cottage and the character of Dorothy and Edward's life there together:

An avenue of tall limes leads across a gently sloping field to the half-acre of land on which their cottage stands. Here the avenue abruptly ends, the last three great trees standing in the little garden and sheltering the Cottage. These limes seem alive with long-tailed tits who build their nests high up among the thick foliage. Below the Cottage, the field slopes abruptly to the water meadow, where the Itchen and all the little streams which flow from and into it wind swiftly and silently amongst great masses of flowering reeds and yellow flags, marsh agrimony and purple loosestrife... The Cottage itself was simple enough, 'a tin cottage' as Dorothy always called it, with its roof painted red, its walls covered with trellis, so that it is buried in creepers, honey-suckle, roses, clematis, amongst which many birds, blackbirds, thrushes, chaffinches, robins, and wagtails build their nests. It was meant only to serve as a necessary shelter, for all real life was lived out of doors, but like everything that Dorothy touched, it has a dainty charm of its own. The little sitting-room with its great window opening down to the ground, has its walls hung with blue linen, and there is a bit of soft blue carpet on the floor. The comfortable chairs and sofa are covered with blue and white chintz, and on the wall are two long rows of books...
Every week end during the early spring and summer was spent at the Cottage, so that they saw the most beautiful season of the year, the time of blossom and promise, at its best. No outsider was allowed to disturb their peace. Dorothy always felt very keenly the strain of social life, she needed complete rest, and felt that the only way in which she could do her duties in the world was by securing a refuge where she could be sure of perfect peace. She determined therefore to enter into no relations with the people of Itchen Abbas and the neighbourhood... She would never have become the woman she was without

---

* Wife of Mandell Creighton who, as the Vicar of Embleton, became Grey's tutor and mentor in the early 1880s; afterwards Bishop of London.

long quiet spaces in her life. Communing with nature did for her what religion does for others. It lifted her out of herself, it made her move among big thoughts, a lonely soul, and yet in touch with the harmonies of nature till she found her place in it and became part of it... On Sundays there was no fishing. In the morning generally a book of *The Prelude* would be read aloud. Wordsworth was their high-priest in the study of nature... When bicycles were introduced it was possible to explore a still further range of country... The best part of their happiness seemed bound up with the Cottage. As Dorothy expressed it, there was 'a great feeling of safeness everywhere about the Cottage.' There she could most easily be herself. She wrote once, 'I am not at all a good London wife, but I know I am a good cottage wife.' Of the character of Dorothy's love for nature a friend writes,* 'I never knew a woman to care so much about the country who patronised it so little; but the meaning in it, and the joy of it, passed readily from her calm, deep realisation into the consciousness of her comrade.'

Perhaps the greatest of our natural history writers was W.H. Hudson – for whom Grey obtained a state pension from Prime Minister Balfour† until Hudson was able to earn a living from his writing. He became a close friend of the Greys and, along with Mrs Creighton, was one of the chosen few allowed to stay at the cottage when the Greys went north in late summer. He describes one such visit during 1900 in his *Hampshire Days*:

They had told me about their cottage, which serves them all the best purposes of a lodge in the vast wilderness... A long field's length away from the cottage is the little ancient, rustic, tree-hidden village. The cottage, too, is pretty well hidden by trees, and has the reed and sedge and grass green valley and swift river before it, and behind and on each side green fields and old untrimmed hedges with a few old oak trees growing both in the hedgerows and the fields. There is also an ancient avenue of limes which leads nowhere and whose origin is forgotten. The ground under the trees is over-grown with long grass and nettles and burdock; nobody comes or goes by it, it is only used by the cattle, the white and roan and strawberry shorthorns that graze in the fields and stand in the shade of the limes on very hot days. Nor is there any way or path to the

---

* See 'Tribute to Dorothy' by Elizabeth Robins (page 166).
† Suceeded his uncle, the Marquess of Salisbury, as Leader of the Conservative party and Prime Minister in July 1902.

cottage; but one must go and come over the green fields, wet or dry. Nothing more—no gravel walks; nor startling scarlet geraniums, no lobelias, no cineraries, no calceolarias, nor other gardeners' abominations to hurt one's eyes and make one's head ache. And no dog, nor cat, nor chick, nor child—only the wild birds to keep one company. They knew how to appreciate its shelter and solitariness; they were all about it, and built their nests amid the green masses of ivy, honeysuckle, Virginia creeper, rose, and wild clematis which covered the trellised walls and part of the red roof with twelve years' luxuriant growth.

The impression we receive of Grey in the *Cottage Book* is that of a fine, upright character: sensitive, deeply religious, close to his wife. He was somewhat enigmatic though. A reluctant politician who greatly preferred life in the country to the noise and stress of city life, he turned down a Privy Councillorship in 1895 so as not to feel himself further drawn into politics. His dislike for political life is nowhere better recorded than in an entry for June 22 1895:

> The Government were beaten on Friday night, and we have spent these days in high hopes of an announcement on Monday, which will bring the end of this terrible time within sight.

He was fit and athletic and, with that strong nose immortalized by the cartoonists, his was a patrician appearance; he was also a fine sportsman, capable of covering vast distances both on foot and by bicycle around the local Hampshire countryside. In 1896, having learnt to play real tennis at Oxford, he even became British Champion at both Lords and Queens. Lord Robert Cecil*, who worked with Grey at the Foreign Office during the war, thought that Grey's greatest asset as Foreign Secretary was his character:

> It was that, too, which at the beginning of the war gained the favourable consideration of the world for our account of the causes which led to the outbreak of hostilities. Europe and other civilised countries were prima facie disposed to accept as true anything Grey said. Where he was in controversy with other countries as to the facts they preferred to believe him. They trusted his veracity and his fairness and even when, later in the war, our blockade operations seemed

---

* Third son of the Marquess of Salisbury, who became Grey's Under-Secretary of State for Foreign Affairs during the war.

inconsistent with neutral rights, foreign countries were ready to believe our proceedings were really essential for our defence, and were not the outcome of arrogant navalism.

His religion was of supreme importance. Trevelyan reports that the passionate feeling of his life was that in the enjoyment of nature lay the greatest good of man. Like Wordsworth, he saw God through nature and his love of birds was an expression of not only his love of Dorothy but also his love of God.

This is confirmed by Grey's own words, writing about spring at the cottage:

> …the beauty has been overwhelming; pear and apple blossom overlapped and the profusion and splendour were more than human capacity could appreciate. I used to feel at this season of the year a sense of waste because I could not enjoy at once all that was spread abroad; till one day the overwhelming egotism of looking at it from this point of view occurred to me, and I thought that God might be contemplating it all. Then I ceased to be oppressed by the sense of waste. The sight of all this beauty and the feeling of response to it in one's self gives assurance that God rules in the universe and that evil cannot prevail.

In one of the most enchanting entries in the *Cottage Book*, for July 2 1894, Dorothy writes:

> The wren sang nearly all morning. We talked about it while we were at break-fast the first morning, and thought how nice it was that we knew enough to be able to love it so much, and how many people there were who would not be ware of it, and E. said, "Fancy if God came in and said, 'did you notice my wren,' and they were obliged to say they did not know it was there."

The *Cottage Book* paints an idyllic picture of Grey's early married life. But at the time of the final entries, tragedy struck. On February 1 1906, Dorothy was thrown from her dogcart near Ellingham in Northumberland. She never regained consciousness. Trevelyan tells us what a profound event in Grey's life this was:

> He had shared with her all his mind, all his happiness, all his pursuits, he had no life but their common life, all had now to be rebuilt on the basis of solitude, and remembrance of things past. Now would be seen how great was his strength, never before tested to the full. He had been awakened from his dream of happiness

with Dorothy amid the woods and the birds, a dream as beautiful as their friend Hudson's imaginings in 'Green Mansions'. Yet it had not been a dream; for long it had been a reality on earth and it lived in his retentive and practised memory. On these terms he was left alone, to face for eleven years a task as grim as any British Statesman has ever had to face. His eyes were grave to sadness, as men saw who looked at him, but the well-springs within were not dry.

It is unfortunate that Dorothy did not contribute more to the *Cottage Book*. Her style is very distinctive, charmingly old-fashioned and poetic. An atmospheric entry for June 27 1899 finds her sleeping outside on a balmy summer's night:

> When a trout jumps and splashes flat it sets all the sedge birds noising... I got the little breeze that says "the dawn—the dawn," and died away.

Perhaps the reason she was not as prolific with her pen as her husband was that she spent more time at the cottage; to her it was a constant home. That she adored the place is clear. 'Dear Hampshire', she says. 'The winter here is much softer than in the north, and it seems much easier for fine days to be warm, and for the sun to get through the clouds.' For a born-and-bred north-erner this is a remarkable conversion.

On May 2 1903 she describes her return from the River Cassley in Sutherland:

> It is wonderful to come here into full spring straight from Rosehall where no spring was. It is like sinking down into a delicious pool.

She felt secure at the cottage, often referring to it as a shelter. A self-absorbed person who actively disliked London society and preferred the solitude of cottage life, it is hard not to believe that it provided her with a form of escapism. Grey on the other hand was an up-and-coming politician, a future Foreign Secretary and much sought after by society hostesses.

Dorothy was also a brilliant observer of nature, completely at ease with the stillness and patience needed to record the activities of wildlife in detail (another reason for regretting her reluctance to contribute more fully to the diary). Grey appreciated this and wrote in the *Cottage Book* during May 1902, 'D. came on Friday and her exploits on Saturday overshadowed everything else', and again, 'The space above is left for D. who should have much to say.'

Although the *Cottage Book* portrays a decade of blissful coexistence, Grey's relationship with Dorothy merits closer examination. There is no doubt that they were devoted to each other and united by their common interests. He was devastated by her early death; it left a deep scar that never healed with time. As late as June 1917 he wrote (from Fallodon) to a friend, Katherine Lyttelton:

> I have had wonderful days here: they make me long terribly to have Dorothy with me; but when I think of all the sad and awful things public and private I should have to tell her, if she came back, the War and all its horrors and grief it has brought to friends' homes, and then the other griefs. And now, of course, the burning of Fallodon would have to be added to the tale. Well, when I think of all this, I feel it selfish and cruel to wish Dorothy back, though I long for it so. It is better to wish that I should go to her.

It is well known that their marriage was *un mariage blanc*. When they returned from their honeymoon, Dorothy told Grey that she had a strong aversion to the physical side of marriage. Dorothy never liked children and had no desire to have any herself. This aspect of their relationship was mentioned in a report sent back to the German Government by their ambassador in London, and Mrs Belloc Lowndes, in her book *A Passing World*, writes:

> Grey told his second wife Pamela, the widow of Lord Glenconner, that after he and Dorothy had been married a considerable number of years she suddenly suggested they should lead a normal married life. He demurred, giving as the reason they were both happy and satisfied with the life they had both agreed on leading.

We have to ask ourselves why he refused the offer of a normal physical relationship with his wife. There seemed no such problems with his second marriage. After they had been married some months, when Pamela was expecting a child – which she subsequently lost – Grey had just turned sixty. He had been close friends with the Glenconners, as can be seen from the *Cottage Book*. But Emma Tennant, Pamela's granddaughter, in her recent book about her family, *Strangers*, states that alongside Grey's close friendship with Eddie Tennant it had been said that Grey conducted a long love affair with Pamela. Pamela's second son, Kit, who was born in 1899, was christened Christopher Grey Tennant and Edward Grey was one of his godparents. After Dorothy's death the three of them certainly spent an enormous amount of time together. The Tennants lived in Queen Anne's Gate, only a few minutes' walk from the

Sir Edward and Lady Grey with a young Winston Churchill and Richard Haldane in 1901
at Guisachan, the home of Lord Tweedmouth* in the Scottish Highlands

Foreign Office. It is interesting to note that all Grey's correspondence with
Pamela mysteriously disappeared after his death in 1933. Lloyd George is said
to have accused Grey, both in public and private, of some scandal in his personal life. This is touched on in Harold Nicolson's diaries†, with an entry for

---

* First Lord of the Admiralty 1906–8 and married to Winston Churchill's aunt, Fanny Spencer
Churchill.
† *The Diaries and letters of Harold Nicolson* 1930–39. Elected National Labour MP for West
Leicester in 1935 and married to poet and novelist Vita Sackville-West.

Trafalgar Day in 1932 when he lunched at Churt with Lloyd George: 'Lloyd George talks of Asquith; his inability to face facts except under pressure. Of Grey; his sham honesty.'

Perhaps it is too much for us to accept the almost saintly image of Grey as portrayed in Trevelyan's biography. Trevelyan was, after all, an intimate friend and kinsman from Northumberland who did not give enough credit to Pamela for the creative influence that she had over a very long period of Grey's life. Nor should we forget that Grey spent many years in the highest echelons of political life – as ruthless and competitive a career as any. To have obtained and held one of the three highest offices of state for more than a decade bespeaks a determination and ambition not apparent in the *Cottage Book*. There is no hint there that this seemingly unambitious, disinterested politician would become celebrated worldwide for his words spoken at the outbreak of the First World War, 'The lights are going out all over Europe. We shall not see them lit again in our lifetime.' Yet there is evidence from his political career that Grey was capable of plotting at the highest level. Just before the Liberals had assumed office, Grey, Asquith and Richard Haldane entered into the 'Relugas Compact' (named after Grey's fishing lodge on the Findhorn) whereby Campbell Bannerman was to be allowed the premiership, but only on the condition that he moved to the House of Lords. The 'Liberal Imperialists' would then control the Commons – Asquith as Leader and Chancellor, Grey as Foreign Secretary, while Haldane became Lord Chancellor. Grey not only felt that Campbell Bannerman did not have the ability to control the House but also he concluded that his old friend and mentor at the Foreign Office, Lord Rosebery, was a non-starter for the premiership. In the event the compact dissolved; Asquith accepted the office of Chancellor when approached on a one-to-one basis by Campbell Bannerman, Haldane followed to the War Office, and so, reluctantly, Grey accepted the Foreign Office. Campbell Bannerman proved his doubters wrong and turned out to be a surprisingly effective Prime Minister. Grey was gentleman enough to except that his judgement had been awry and wrote as much in personal correspondence to the new Prime Minister.

Foreign affairs under the Conservative Government during the period when the *Cottage Book* was written were characterized by strained relations with two future allies: Russia over their war with Japan (the occupation of Port Arthur) and France over the Fashoda Incident. Relations with Germany grew stiffer by the day with the Kaiser's over-reaction to the Jameson Raid in South

Sir Edward Grey, Foreign Secretary, 1910

Africa* and their aggressive new policy of naval expansion. The most significant event was the Boer War, which commenced in 1899. Grey and his fellow Liberal Imperialists – Asquith, Haldane and Rosebery – supported the Conservative Government's war policy and it was this small group of brilliant politicians that so attracted the young Winston Churchill, shortly to cross the floor of the House over tariff reform.

Following the Liberal landslide at the polls and Dorothy's death, Grey threw himself into his work at the Foreign Office. For the next nine years he attempted to keep the peace in Europe and tried to draw Britain out of its past isolationism. The cornerstone of his policy was entente with France and a continuation of the long-standing British policy of maintaining the balance of power in Europe – by allying with the weaker powers against the stronger. To this end he implemented an agreement with France, initially drawn up in 1904 by his predecessor Lord Lansdowne. In January 1906 he opened 'Military Conversations'† with French army chiefs in the event of a war with Germany. Agreements followed with Russia in 1907 and Japan in 1911. At all times Grey determined to build a strong relationship with America and to this end he developed a close friendship with both President Wilson's special adviser on Foreign Affairs, Colonel House, and the American ambassador in London, Walter Page.

Most people attribute the forging of our 'special relationship' with the USA to Winston Churchill and President Franklin Roosevelt. However, it was presaged a generation earlier between Sir Edward Grey and Franklin's cousin, Theodore Roosevelt, who were brought together through their mutual love of birds. Theodore Roosevelt had just ended two terms as President of the USA and was on a world tour that concluded in England.

---

* The Transvaal mining boom of the 1880s had brought in a large number of British and European immigrants called Uitlanders. The Boers, feeling threatened, had restricted their civil rights. On December 29 1885, Dr Jameson of the British South Africa Company led 500 men into the Transvaal, hoping to take Johannesburg. The raid proved a disaster, and they were captured by the Boers. The Kaiser rashly sent a telegram to President Kruger congratulating him on maintaining his country's independence, which caused a storm of protest in Britain.
† These took place between the French and British Chiefs of Staff, commencing in January 1906, to discuss joint war preparations in the event of a sudden German attack on France. Although Grey was later criticized for not obtaining cabinet approval at the time, his action led to the Haldane Army Reforms and formation of the Expeditionary Force vital to British survival in 1914.

Pamela Tennant, Sir Edward Grey's second wife, in 1907 with her children, left to right, Clare, Christopher, Stephen and Bim

Before taking the boat home from Southampton, Roosevelt specifically asked to be taken for a woodland walk to enjoy the birdsong. There was no better guide for him than the British Foreign Secretary. On the morning of June 9 1910, having taken the train from Waterloo, the two men walked down the Itchen valley from the little village of Tichborne to the cottage, a few miles downstream. From here they moved on into the heart of the New Forest. During their walk they saw forty-one different species of bird and heard the songs of twenty-three of them. They discussed politics and poetry. The two men became firm friends and remained so for the rest of their lives.

Grey and his close friend Richard Haldane can claim much of the credit for Britain's state of readiness when war finally came in 1914. At the War Office, Haldane had been responsible for far-reaching army reforms, and Grey had been the most constant supporter of keeping the Dreadnought building programme ahead of that of the German navy. After a masterful speech by Grey at the House of Commons, war was declared on August 3 1914. *The Times* wrote in Grey's obituary some twenty years later that he was 'the diplomatist thanks to whom the pure and honourable character of our motives for the most momentous decision of a hundred years was made generally manifest'. Hugh Cecil* wrote of 'the great dignity, warm emotion and perfect taste of Grey's speech', adding that 'all these substantial merits set off by his wonderful manner go to make his speech the greatest example of the art of persuasion that I have ever listened to'.

II

When Grey acquired the plot of land from his cousin Lord Northbrook, and built his home beside the Itchen in 1890, he intended to use it as a fishing cottage. It is interesting to note that fishing is only mentioned once in the *Cottage Book* and that was on June 25 1900 when Grey disturbed a turtle-dove while landing a trout. The reader would hardly guess that as an all-round fisherman Grey was bettered by none. Mrs Creighton in her *Memoir of Dorothy* wrote:

---

* Fifth son of the Marquess of Salisbury and leader of the 'Hooligans', a group of well-born, dissident young Tories that included Winston Churchill, Arthur Stanley and Lord Percy. Hugh Cecil was best man at Winston's wedding to Clementine.

Every year in the spring and early summer Edward fished on the Itchen, then when the glory of the woods in the south of England was over, when the water meadows seem to grow a little too soft, the air to lack freshness, the ever flowing chalk stream so clear and so docile and perfectly under control, seemed just a little tame, they would go to the far north of Scotland and fish the rough noisy streams and great brown pools clearing after a flood.

Grey then would take his wet fly to such famous salmon rivers as the Helmsdale, Lochy, Findhorn and Cassley. The Greys would stay at Rosehall on the Cassley and in *Fly Fishing* he writes:

> The best days I had personally on the Cassley were in the latter part of April 1911. Heavy showers kept the river up for nine continuous fishing days and in the first eight of them I caught forty-four salmon.

In the same book he relates how the best day's sea trout fishing was when he caught twenty-two fish on the little River Fleet in Sutherland, 'when the water was not very high and there was a gloomy gale from the east in August'.

He wrote *Fly Fishing* in 1898, aged thirty, and the book represents one of the finest texts on fly fishing ever written – certainly the equal of Izaak Walton's *Compleat Angler*. Much of it must have been written at the cottage. When he edited a second edition in 1930 he admitted that the best of his dry-fly fishing days were already over by 1898, as within a few years his eyesight would begin to deteriorate. He tells of a memorable day, in the third week of July 1892, when he caught six brace of trout on the Itchen, weighing twenty-four pounds.

The *Cottage Book* was never intended as a diary of his sporting exploits. It was dedicated to the birds, flowers and trees that shared and enhanced the couple's life there. It was to record the joy and happiness Edward and Dorothy derived from nature; to celebrate 'Beech Sunday' or 'Lilac Sunday'. However, what the *Cottage Book* did eventually provide was a huge bank of memories that Grey would draw upon, many years later, when he wrote his finest book, *The Charm of Birds*.

Grey was also a lifelong railway enthusiast. While compiling the *Cottage Book* he had become a professional railway man. Aside from the odd reference to the little branch line station of Itchen Abbas, the reader can be forgiven for not drawing this conclusion. It is not surprising that he was fascinated by steam trains. The main line on the London and North Eastern Railway passed close to Fallodon. By an agreement under which the railway was built Grey had a right to stop trains at the little station at the bottom of his drive.* Seton Gordon, the famous Scottish naturalist, in his book *Edward Grey and His Birds* tells how Grey liked to take an unsuspecting guest to the side of the local signal box and watch him jump as the Northern Express rushed by, and that 'Lord Grey told me that he and his brother, when they were younger, often timed the expresses over that particular stretch of line going north, and they found that the trains usually travelled at a speed of 75 miles an hour'.

In 1898 Grey became a Director of the North Eastern Railway. Trevelyan describes how, 'twice a month they met at York, dining pleasantly together overnight at the Station Hotel and transacting their business the next morning'. In 1904 he was elected Chairman with a salary of £2000 per year. In March 1899 he wrote to Dorothy from his hotel of a walk taken following a Board meeting:

> I have had a walk alone in a fine March wind and sun up the Ouse, and watched the ripples and wondered whether I could have put a salmon fly as far as the opposite bank, and at last I came to quite open country, larger than Battersea Park, with no people, and felt as having seen the wide fields and free sky I had looked God in the face and been refreshed and I thought I would write and tell you.

This vividly demonstrates Grey's sense of the close links between religion and nature. But he was, essentially, a Victorian figure who found some difficulty in coping with the adjustments imposed by a changing, more modern world. In the new edition of *Fly Fishing* published in 1930, Grey looked back on the days of the *Cottage Book* and considered the changes that had taken place in the Itchen valley:

> The cottage that I put up by the Itchen in 1890 was intended only as a fishing cottage; a place in which to get food, sleep, and shelter when I was not fishing. It became a sanctuary. The peace and beauty of the spot made it a sacred place. Great changes, however, had been taking place that were inseparable from a new epoch. For the first fifteen years there was little change and had been little change for many years before this time. I had seen the old mill at the village not far away replaced by a new building, and the dull, monotonous sound of a turbine had

---

* Lady Alethea Eliot, Grey's god-daughter, recalls how he never over-exploited this 'feudal right'. 'The Flying Scotsman' only ground to a halt when Grey was a cabinet minister.

replaced the lively splashing of the waterwheel; but otherwise things remained as they were. The cottage was invisible from any road; it was approached by an old lime avenue, long disused, and the track down this was not suited for any wheels but those of a farm cart. There was a little wayside station on a single railway line close by; but the quickest route from London was to go by a fast train to Winchester, and thence to drive a distance between four and five miles to the nearest point to the cottage that was accessible by wheels. This was a drive of at least half an hour in a one-horse fly. Presently taxi-cabs took the place of the horse conveyance and reduced the time of the drive to a quarter of an hour. Was this an advantage? On balance it was not. For escape from London meant that hurry, noise and bustle had been left behind: I had entered unto leisure, where saving of time was no object, and often I would walk from Winchester to enjoy the country. There was a foot-path way on each side of the river. By one of these one entered the cottage without, except for the momentary crossing of one road and of three secluded lanes, having had touch or sight of a road. There were thirty-three stiles on this path. There was much charm in this midnight walk. Traffic had ceased, cottage lights had been put out, the inmates were all at rest or asleep. Now and then one heard in passing the song of a nightingale or a sedgewarbler, but in the main there was silence. It was pleasant after the hardness of London streets and pavements to feel the soft dust about my feet. On a still summer night there were sweet and delicate scents in the air, breathed forth from leaves and herbs and grass, and from the earth itself. It was as if one's own very being was soothed and in some way refined by the stillness, the gentleness and the sweetness of it all. Then came the age of motors and tarred roads. Few people, I imagine, seek the smell of tar for its own sake. To me there is nothing unclean or nauseous in it, but it is a coarse, rough smell. The sweet and delicate scents of the night were obliterated by it, as if, overpowered and repelled, they had sunk back into the leaves and earth from which they had ventured into air. The strong smell of the tar seemed to disturb even the stillness of the night: the soft dust was no more, and the road was hard as a paved street. Not all, but much of the charm of the night walk was gone. There were other changes too; small houses of the villa type were built along the road that was nearest to the cottage: doubtless there are more of them now, for the cottage was accidentally destroyed by fire in January 1923, and I have not seen the place for some years. The sense of change was in the air. It may be that change is for the good:

> *The old order changeth, yielding place to new,*
> *And God fulfils himself in many ways,*
> *Lest one good custom should corrupt the world.*

It is not for us, who cannot foresee the future, who perhaps cannot rightly understand the present, to chide or to repine too much. Only it is impossible for us, who in our youth gave our affections to things that are passed or passing away, to transfer our affections to new things in which a new generation finds delight. The beauty, however, of chalk-stream valleys still remains wonderful. The river still waters meadows that are unspoilt and unchanged, and its clear purity is guarded and protected.

> *Still glides the stream and shall for ever glide,*
> *The form remains, the function never dies.*

Grey's prose style may seem old-fashioned but he was a surprisingly modern and far-sighted man, a pioneer conservationist and ecologist. His last speech in the House of Lords was on February 14 1933, and was a plea for controlling the oil spillage from ships:

My Lords, I do not wish for a moment to minimize the terrible effect of oil pollution on birdlife, which has been so forcibly put by your Lordships. But there is one other aspect of the matter I would like to bring forward. One of the famous tributes in our literature to our sea is that it performs the work of preventing the pollution of our shores.

> *The moving waters at their priestlike task*
> *Of pure ablution round earth's human shores.*   KEATS

Is all this to come to an end? Apart from what oil pollution does to the birds, it is a horrible thought from our point of view that our shores should be filthy. We are really proud of our sea, and rely upon the Government to take some action if possible to prevent it.

In 1928 Grey became Chancellor of his old university and the work of the Oxford Preservation Trust particularly interested him. Trevelyan wrote:

He was deeply interested in the preservation of the beauty of Oxford and of its rural scenery that he loved so well in his idle youth; and he had equally at heart the rearguard action waged on a wider front by the National Trust, in defence of the wounded beauty of all England. His connection with that body was so close that in 1924 a new post of Vice President was specially created for him.

Grey joined the Royal Society for the Protection of Birds in 1893, becoming a vice-president in the year the *Cottage Book* commenced. In 1919 he chaired the committee to review the Wild Birds Protection Act. Dorothy became a life member in 1895, at the suggestion of her friend W.H. Hudson. She wrote to him:

> I have no feathers except ostrich feathers for the last ten years and have induced several people to give up aigrettes*. I will take more trouble now, and get them to join the Society.

Aside from an abrupt ending there is no hint from the text of the *Cottage Book* that tragedy would rain down on Grey's shoulders in later life. Pamela died in 1928 and Grey retired to Fallodon comforted, no doubt, by his memories and his treasured wildfowl collection. In the same year his brother Charles was killed by a buffalo in Africa, following on from the loss of his brother, George, who was also killed while big game hunting, this time by a lion. His nephew Adrian Graves was killed fighting on the Western Front in 1918. Grey wrote to his sister on Adrian's death:

> It is difficult in these dark days not to become disheartened and discouraged. I find that what helps me most is watching the stability of nature and the orderly procession of the seasons.

It was those happy days at the cottage that prepared him to cope with the stresses of office and the personal tragedies he was to suffer in middle age.

Fallodon was burnt down in 1917 and rebuilt after the war. The cottage suffered a similar fate in 1923 with the only evidence of its presence today the ruins of a brick chimney and a few foundation stones. Trevelyan wrote, 'It became part of Edward Grey's life that every person with whom he desired to make a home with for life was doomed to die, and that every habitation in which he loved to dwell was burnt to the ground.' On top of it all, his eyesight deteriorated rapidly in his latter years as Foreign Secretary.

In July 1916, as a result of increasing blindness, he accepted a peerage and moved to the Lords. In December, eleven years to the day that Grey had been appointed Foreign Secretary, the Asquith Government broke up, replaced by Lloyd George's coalition. Grey retired from public life. He had

---

* White plumes from an egret.

served his constituents loyally for over thirty years, and as a senior minister had selflessly denied concerns for his health and eyesight in the quest for a satisfactory solution to the European conflict. Thus Grey entered the final stage of his life unable to see his beloved birds or to fish accurately with a dry fly. In the introduction to his biography of Grey, Trevelyan wrote:

> He was indeed one whom fortune loved and hated out of common measure. All that he enjoyed so intensely and suffered so profoundly, all that he undertook and endured and performed, operating on a mind and body of unusual strength, made him a nobler man every year he lived. His full spiritual stature had not been reached when he reluctantly took office in December 1905. Two months later his wife died, and his nature grew under the pressure of private sorrow and public care. His face, in youth beaked and bright-eyed like a hawk's, became like that of the king of birds. Men spoke of his 'sad eagle eyes.' At the close of his life all who were sensitive to the touch of greatness felt it in his presence.

The *Cottage Book* remains a charming testament 'to the happiness which on balance outweighed the sadness' in the life of a remarkable, but now mostly forgotten English statesman. When a friend wrote to Grey he epitomized the beauty of this exquisite document:

> I love the way the book begins and ends. It is like a cloud which comes out of nothing into a summery, hazy heaven and as softly disappears.

1894

MARCH 3 TO NOVEMBER 19

TICHBORNE CHURCH
THE VILLAGE LIES ABOUT FOUR MILES FROM THE SOURCE OF THE
ITCHEN AND WAS WHERE GREY COMMENCED HIS FAMOUS 'BIRD WALK' WITH
THEODORE ROOSEVELT IN JUNE 1910

MARCH 3 TO 5.

E. A pair of long-tailed tits haunting the trees in front of the cottage.

MARCH 17 TO 19.

E. The long-tailed tits busy building a nest high up in the end lime tree. A warm early spring, but very dry since February. Saw one wheatear on the downs towards Telegraph*.

APRIL 7 TO 9.

E. Long-tailed tits look at their nest† casually as if they partly wondered what it was. Blackthorn is in splendid flower: at a distance it looks as if the hawthorn must be out. Weather is sunny and so warm that we have not lit the stove at all. Thermometer rose to 69 in the shade on Sunday, but the drought is beginning to be oppressive: it promises to be as disastrous as it was last year. On Saturday I walked out from Winchester in the afternoon and saw wheatears, a redstart, a whinchat, and heard my first willow wren.

We heard two kingfishers making a great noise behind a willow blown up by the roots at the other side of the meadow opposite the cottage. On Monday, after I had gone to London, D. found the nest and saw small fish brought to the hole: she says that only one bird feeds and that the other watches. We found a thrush's nest with eggs and D. watched a chaffinch building by the Aquarium††. A hen chaffinch sings constantly in the poplars in front: its song begins like a chaffinch, but is quite distinct: less robust and finished and not the least like at the end: the bird is apparently paired and the cock seems to think that all is right. There is a great hum of bees in the willows. We saw and heard a cuckoo.

Song Thrush's nest

* Telegraph Hill, just south of the A272 to the east of Chilcomb.
† There is a charming description of the nest in *The Fallodon Papers* (see Grey's address 'The Pleasure in Nature'). He states, 'I have been told that the feathers used in the lining of a long-tailed tit's nest have been counted to number more than nine hundred.'
†† Name given to a part of the river where every trout was visible. Almost certainly under the iron bridge at the east end of the Avington lake.

APRIL 28 TO 30.

E. I came by the last train on Friday night the 27th, and walked out from Winchester, at midnight. It was warm and soft: I heard a nightingale, and one sedge warbler was singing within hearing of the road just where a piece of the river could be seen, light at the end of a little dark path. I walked with my hat off and once a little soft rain fell amongst my hair: there were great forms of leafy trees and a smell and spirit everywhere and I felt the soft country dust about my feet.

There has been rain off and on for the last fortnight, and I have never seen the country look so well: the grass is early and thick, chestnuts heavy with leaves and flowers, beeches bright green, limes half out and some oaks yellow: there are small dark green tufts of leaves even on the ashes and a few sprays of hawthorn open enough to smell. Our cottage room is full of lilac, smelling most sweet, and outside the smell of sweetbriar* is all alive, playing a sort of hide-and-seek unawares with one's nose as it always does. On Saturday I fished at Chilland†; the air was full of the sound of birds, mostly blackbirds, all day: there were a few loud peals of thunder, some short, heavy showers, dense black clouds, and bright gleams of light falling on new leaves in Avington Park††. In the evening we went in the wild park and found many nightingales at the top of it. One thing that struck us was the little

Long-tailed Tit

way that a nightingale's voice will carry compared to the loudness of it close at hand. At some three yards off it was deafening, but at a few yards further the peculiar concentrated loudness was gone, and I think it could not be heard nearly so far off as a blackbird's whistle. A nightingale's song is the most wonderful, but the most imperfect, of songs. The long notes are divine, but they come seldom, and never go on long enough: the song continually breaks out with a burst, which promises a fine full spell, but it is always broken off in the most disappointing way. A blackcap's song, which comes next in quality, is short enough, but it seems finished in a way that no part of the nightingale's ever does, and one can't help thinking with some satisfaction of a good, steady old thrush singing

---

* Similar to the dog rose but rarer with darker pink petals.
† Tiny hamlet just downstream of the cottage.
†† The home of Grey's cousin Lord Northbrook across the water-meadows from the cottage.

Nightingale

right through from the beginning of February to the middle of June.

A blackbird has built in the alcove, a large nest, which is really fixed on at the bottom, but it looks as if it was barely balanced in the honeysuckle, and had been put there for a joke: the first egg was laid this morning. A chaffinch has built in the traveller's joy above my window: the nest had two eggs yesterday and three to-day: it is left unfinished on the side next the iron, and as it gets the full after-noon sun the eggs and bird will surely be roasted. The chaffinch by the Aquarium has made a very good nest, and is sitting. There is a wren with eggs in the wren path*, another sitting in the "Hiddin"†, and a chaffinch with eggs there also. A greenfinch with three eggs in a bush in the field, blackbirds everywhere, and the thrush which had eggs has now three fine young birds nearly fledged. A brood of young robins is well on the wing: the kingfishers are about their nest, but so many that we can't find out what they are doing.

MAY 5 TO 7.

E. Down to breakfast on Saturday: early morning distinctly cold; both days fine but never warm. Blackbird and chaffinch on sides of cottage both sitting: greenfinch's nest in the field destroyed: eggs broken and nests rumpled, but a nest which was unfinished last week has now five reed bunting's eggs, and I saw the cock bird on them on Sunday. Three wren nests in or near wren path, two of them hanging over water, one at the very tip of the boughs of the big chestnut, so that it is well over the lake. The other is fixed in the boarded side of a hatch†† in the field, so that there is no foothold anywhere outside the nest. D. has found two robins' nests, a bullfinch with five splendid green eggs, well spotted, and one nest unfinished and unknown. No news of the kingfishers, but on Sunday I heard a great tapping in a poplar close to the cottage. I could see no bird, but a new round hole in a dead branch caught my

* A favourite walk of the Greys running along the north side of Avington lake and much frequented by singing wrens.
† A concealed brook to the north of Avington lake much frequented by kingfishers.
†† Part of the irrigation system in the water-meadows.

Children in the Post Office garden at Tichborne

eye, and when I came back to it after walking round the tree, I saw something like a small face in the middle of it. I had the glasses ready, and saw the head of a lesser spotted woodpecker with a crimson crown clearly. Later on D. and I watched the hen bird with no crimson crown clearing out masses of sawdust, till at last we went too near and it flew away.

D. I stayed till the afternoon, and spent all morning in the wild park*, which is in a lovely state of light green beauty. I sat down by each nightingale and listened to it till it stopped, then went on to the next, and so on. I had been listening for about an hour when I heard a very slight sibilant sound that reminded me of a wood wren†. I went to it but heard nothing, and went back to my nightingale. After a bit I heard it

Bullfinch's nest

* The heavily planted north-western fringes of the lake.
† Wood wren; better known as a wood warbler. Its song is described by Grey in *The Charm of Birds*: 'The bird has in fact two songs, so distinct and unlike that nothing but clear and close view can convince one that the different sounds are made by the same bird.'

Wood Warbler

again louder, and went and sat under the oak where it was. I heard little whisperings high up, and at last came a good long sibilant note which made me feel very happy, because it was certainly a wood wren, and wood wrens are much loved. I saw the bird, only one, and it sang at intervals of about four minutes very faintly generally, and there were none of the staccato notes which generally go before sibilant sound. I heard none of the long notes either, but the sibilant notes got stronger as they went on and the rest will follow. It worked about in the oak all the time I was with it, about an hour, and I left it there, hoping to find it again on Saturday.

The nightingales have spread all over the east side of the park; they are by the saw-mills*, and right up in the corner where the blue-bells are. They seem to sing more continuously now than when they first came, which makes the song more satisfactory than when there were such long intervals between the notes. I have looked three times at the lesser spotted's hole, and waited about ten minutes each time, but have not seen it. I suppose the nest hole is enough scraped out. Tiny showers came now and then in the morning, like spray from a fountain. I found three wren nests lined but with no eggs, and one chaffinch sitting.

MAY 19.

E. We came early on the 11th for a Whitsuntide holiday, and, except from Saturday evening to Monday morning, when we were at Stratton, we have been here since. The long-tailed tits, which were building in March, did not bring the young ones out till the 17th of May. D. found them all in a row on a branch in the hedge, except one weakling, which was in the grass calling. There were nine altogether; we caught the weak one and fed it with flies and aphids. It had no fear, but no idea of feeding itself, and we think it certainly lost the others and died. The reed bunting's nest has been robbed, but the others are all right, and the blackbird and chaffinch on the cottage hatched last Monday and are doing well. We found that the kingfisher's nest has a hole at the back, through which we could see about seven eggs, and I got one out

* At the extreme eastward end of Avington lake by the junction with the river.

with a bit of stick to look at. This must be the second lot of eggs, and we presume the first brood was got safely away. Chestnuts are still covered with flower, and so is the hawthorn, but the flower of both is falling: the hawthorn may be said to have reached its best at the middle of the month. Laburnum is fully out and lilac nearly over. The success of our garden so far has been a clump of purple iris. No roses yet.

We have had some rain, but not much: sixty-four has been the highest shade temperature, but the evenings have been warm, and on at least three days this week we have sat out of doors comfortably till nine o'clock. To-day has turned cold, with a N.E. wind: temperature 46 at ten o'clock this morning, and less at sunset. We have had to fold up our table and light the stove, and the leaves are shivering outside.

MAY 21.

E. My holiday is at an end, and we are going back to London. It is very cold. Yesterday (Sunday) the thermometer never got above 45, and fell to 34 at night. D. went into the wild park to hear the nightingales at midnight. There was a full moon, and the grass was stiff with frost.

JUNE 2.

D. It rained hard in London when we started, but was warmer than it had been for a fortnight. The lesser spotted woodpeckers are feeding, and they are in very bad plumage and looked hard worked. They won't feed if we stand nearer than the walnut tree in the ditch. Both birds feed; they cling on outside the hole and dab their heads in; there is a slight young bird noise to be heard when one stands close underneath the nest. The cotton nest in the withy bed is empty and soaked, and has a few dead leaves in it, evidently deserted, and we shall never know who built it. I found two willow wrens' nests in the wild park near the saw-mill on Saturday, and took E. to see them on Sunday. We saw a parter* quite flat and spread out under one of the thorn trees which we had passed under twice. The parter let us go

Kingfisher's eggs

* An English partridge.

The village pub at Tichborne around the turn of the century

quite close and look at it, and evidently thought it was not found. We sat on a peeled oak in the sun for some time and listened to the last two or three nightingales. We had been there about twenty minutes when I was ware of a nightingale slinking out of a bramble close by us. I looked and found the nest with four youngs in it. It was built of dead leaves shuffled together, and a thick lining of skeleton leaves held them together. I looked for more, but only found one more willow wren. On Sunday morning E., who was coming out of the chalk pit*, met a robin with food coming from our black gate. We thought we might as well see where it went and waited, and when both birds had very cautiously fed, we looked amongst the roots of the lime which stands outside the railing, and found a large young cuckoo in their nest. It heaved up and down when we looked at it and pecked very savagely, and opened its huge scarlet throat. We fed it with

Willow Warbler's nest

* A small chalk quarry on the east side of the lime avenue approaching the cottage, which had become a favoured nesting site for many warblers.

hard-boiled egg, which it learned to eat after a bit, and we teased it a good deal. It was very soft and gray, and had nice eyes and a spotted tail. The kingfisher's eggs seem to be hatched, as pieces of shell are in the nest, but we could not see any young. There are many kingfishers to be seen up and down the river. E. saw three under the chestnut in the wren path, and I put up several as I came along it. They can nearly always be heard going up and down the hidden brook. There has been cold weather ever since we left, and no roses out except three Idéals on the house, some gloires, and the row of pink chinas in front, which look very nice and bright. The creepers on the house and the sweet-briar have grown more this year than any since they were planted. There are far more long-tailed than any other kind of tit about here. Wren path is full of them. The second brood of sparrows is in the corner of my room under the roof, and the young sparrows which were hatched in ivy on the walnut are now helping to feed that second brood. I have seen a cuckoo bird's-nesting. It perched on small blackthorn bushes and looked inside each one.

It rained hard Sunday night and thundered, and there was much rain on Monday, but it was warm. Thermometer 60 most of the day, though no sun.

JUNE 17 (SUNDAY).

E. We came yesterday. There has been a long spell of cold weather since it turned cold on the 19th of May: the frost then was a notable frost and did a great deal of damage all over the country. Up to the middle of April this was a very forward year, now it is backward in some respects: for instance it is very difficult to get strawberries: we had two baskets this time, but they were a very scratch lot and seemed foreign. The roses have begun, but we have not got to the big blow yet of anything, except chinas. There is not a single white moss rose out, so they at any rate are four weeks later than last year.

The honeysuckle is just beginning. Yesterday was in some ways perfect. It was not hot, only up to 65, but there was plenty of sun and little wind: it was just warm enough to sit out and the place seemed full of summer. To-day has been

Kingfisher with 'Grey's bridge' in the background

Honeysuckle

cloudy, cool, and damp; temperature about 55 for most of the day, and the windows have been shut a good deal: on the corresponding day last year it was over 80 and I saw the pheasant drink. The young cuckoo flies about the chalk pit and makes a noise. We saw young nightingales in the nightingale place, to the great distress of the old birds. The singing of all birds is less and the songs that are heard are languid.

JUNE 24 (SUNDAY).

E. No hot weather. The temperature never went below 57 last night, but it was 58 at three in the afternoon, and has never been above 62 on either of these days.

The big blow of roses does not seem any nearer, but the honeysuckle is very gay, though the best of it has yet to come. The aphis has destroyed all the bloom on the west side of the house as usual, but the other is clean and splendid. A few pink moss rose buds, but no white ones showing colour yet: the latter were much earlier than the pink last year. Wild roses are fully out; there were a good many last week: the elderflower is thick. A spotted fly-catcher was haunting the cottage with a long wisp in its beak this morning, and later on I saw it get into the chaffinch's old nest and be very busy for a few moments, and be very annoyed when it saw me. There is a new reed warbler's nest in the wren path, but nothing in it. The birds have sung rather more this time, especially blackcaps, chiffchaffs, wrens, and thrushes, hardly any blackbirds.

JULY 1.

E. Two hot days. To-day it has been 83 in the shade, and yesterday it was 78, though there was a strong east wind. The week has been fine too, and the great blow of roses has come. The white moss are ahead of the pink after all, but the Gem are ahead of both. We have enjoyed both days immensely. When we arrived there was one wren singing most noticeably round the cottage; as I looked out it flew happily over the cottage from the poplars to the limes, singing as it passed over the roof: "like a blessing" D. said when I told her. It sang nearly all day yesterday and to-day, always near us some-where. To-day as I was waking the first thing I was aware of was a blackcap's song*: I knew of it for some time before I was properly awake: it too sang nearly all day close round us. Both these birds were still in full song, and it seemed as if they were a special gift to us—a parting one perhaps before all songs cease for the season. The woods are nearly silent, and it was very strange and sweet to have these two birds singing as loud and more constantly than any birds had been noticed to sing before. We sat out the whole day, till sunset, when we went for a walk in the meadows. D. planted some Test musk which F. Lubbock[†] had sent her, and I bathed. The spotted flycatchers really have turned the old chaffinch nest into a spotted flycatcher's: there are four eggs and the bird is sitting, but flies off whenever we look round the corner.

JULY 2.

D. It rained a little now and then in the morning but was warm, 76 and a south wind. The wren sang nearly all morning. We talked about it while we were at breakfast the first morning, and thought how nice it was that we knew enough to be able to love it so much, and how many people there were who would not be ware of it, and E. said, "Fancy if God came in and said, 'did you notice my wren,' and they were obliged to say they did not know it was there." The nest we thought was a reed warbler has now five sedge eggs in it.

JULY 8 (SUNDAY).

E. Two very different days from the last. Highest temperature 65. Wild roses and sweet-briar are going over, privet is out. There was rain this evening, which was very timely, as the hay has been got in. Our roses are finer even than last Sunday: a very great quantity are out and Baroness R. and La France are very large. We went a walk this afternoon and crossed the valley from Itchen Stoke[††] to Ovington by the river path, and watched a man fishing in the broad, shallow river, amongst tall reeds and deep weeds. The Ayrshire rose is in very fine flower.

Wren

---

* This revival of song is very noticeable, probably because of its quality and strength, and is described by Grey in *The Charm of Birds* in the chapter titled 'From Full to Least Song'.
† Maybe the wife of Liberal MP Sir John Lubbock.
†† A village two miles upstream of the cottage.

JULY 15 (SUNDAY).

E. Not warm again: 63 has been the highest on both days. The great blow of roses is over, but there are quite enough left to stock our room well, and we find a few special tea roses every week, which give great delight. The spotted flycatcher has hatched, and a large white lily is out, but the thing to attend to is the limes: they are in splendid flower, the best we have ever seen, it is thought, and numbers of bees hum there all day long. The flowers look so heavy with honey and make the trees look luscious and light. It's a pity that the weather has not been warmer and stiller. We went a new walk to-day and found Burrage Farm and the deep lane.

JULY 16.

D. I did not go up till four. It poured all day and temperature was 57. Also wind blew strongly but did not prevent the wren from singing. I cut off dead rose heads and was in nearly all day.

JULY 22 (SUNDAY).

E. Not much sun either day and never above 65. The lime flower is just beginning to turn brown and has lost its fresh beauty, but the bees are there as much as ever and the air is full of its scent. The hum of bees, if one listens, seems to be always growing greater. A thrush sang this evening and was attended to: the wren is faithful still: the young spotted flycatchers have got feathers: a robin has been feeding its young ones on the lawn: and four young goldfinches, the parent flycatchers, a young robin and a chiffchaff all sat in a row at once on the fence. Numbers of wagtails (pied) in the reed bed this evening. Not many roses, but several white moss: had the last strawberries.

AUGUST 5.

E. Rather windy and not above 64. A little kind warm rain fell at dusk to-night and I sat and had my tea in it. The flycatcher's nest is empty and young flycatchers sit on the fence and in the rose bed and peck and take little flights of independence. Travellers' joy is in full flower. Rather more roses again and many buds, but the want of sun makes it difficult for many of the tea

Water Lilies

Children beside the river at Itchen Stoke; note the reed-cutter with the scythe

roses to open and the wet has made many buds sodden. Some fine flowers of Archduchess Marie Immaculata gave D. great pleasure. No bird sang except the wren*: the next most noticeable sound is the twitter of green-finches. Harvest in full swing.

AUGUST 13.

E. A Monday has been added to the usual Saturday and Sunday, and it has been a glorious day; bright and windy and getting warmer, up to 66. One felt very grateful to have a long spell of sunlight again. Of roses the Archduchess has surpassed herself, and D. and I both consider that some half-dozen blooms of it are the finest thing we have ever seen in roses. The Lonicera still flowers, but the scent is not nearly so strong as that of the earlier flowers. Not many other roses, some Adam and La France and Madame Hoste. The wren sang very seldom and very faintly, the finches are all off to the corn, which is being cut fast, but spotted flycatchers

Reed Warbler on nest

* The quietest month of the birdsong year; many birds are in moult after nesting.

49

Carting maize at Tichborne

abound, and one is aware of them everywhere. D. saw four kingfishers one after the other below the Jaw Hatches[*], and we saw others in different places. On Sunday we saw a a cock redstart, moulting but handsome, at Tichborne[†]. On Sunday afternoon we went a long and successful walk; we started at 12.30 and were not back till after five. We went by Chilland and up outside the long strip: then we followed the Cheriton road, and sat for a bit on the high bare downs: it was cloudy and a wind swept over us and we looked down on to many fields, some of corn with the wind sweeping over them. Close to us were numbers of bright little flowers of many colours dancing in the turf: then we went down and up again through the juniper place to the beech gate, where we got into woodland once more, and came down a funny rough grass strip between hedges to the pond farm, then another quaint rough road, a grass field and so to the chestnut-tree house, and Tichborne and into thick woodland and water meadows. From Tichborne we found a curious path over the hill to Ovington, and

Cock Redstart

[*] Two sluices 500 yards downstream of the cottage, which formed a small island in the form of a human jaw. They were part of the irrigation system for the water-meadows.
[†] A village four miles upstream of Itchen Abbas.

at Ovington we had milk and biscuits at the Bush Inn: then back to the river path and Itchen Stoke—along the road and home in rain for the last mile. It was a fine varied walk, the bare, open, dry country with its puddled ponds to catch the rain-water, the common woodland and isolated farms—all without streams or running water—and then the Itchen valley with long grass and reeds and numbers of streams, a village every mile, and large woods and parks at intervals.

AUGUST 19.

E. Leave-taking* Sunday. D. came early on Saturday and fished, but I could not get away till the last train and got here about midnight, after a moonlight drive from Winchester, thinking all the way of my walk out along the same road in April at the same time of night and how nice it all is. Practically a whole summer has come and gone since that walk, and this place has been to us all and more than we ever hoped it would be. In taking leave of it, one takes leave of the summer too. The day has been full of thoughtful last looks: here and there some place or tree is lit, as one looks at it, by a happy memory, like a gleam of light falling on it. We went by the wren path, where there was a common coarse grass in exquisite flower, a soft sort of pale colour with a very faint blend of green: there was a great stretch of it like a sort of milky way under dark green trees. From there we went up the withy bed where the reeds in places meet far above one's head; up the deep lane to Burrage Farm and back by the wild park nightingale path, remembering bits of what had been. Spotted flycatchers meet one's eye everywhere: a large flock of sandmartins were on the telephone wires close to the cottage—off and on all day in numbers: they seem to be on the move and I saw the last swift. Windy, cloudy, damp and cool, never above 62 all day.

There has been some rain almost every Sunday this summer: we have only had one hot one and on no other day has the thermometer reached 70 or near it. But what does it matter in comparison with a bad drought, which we were fearing again in the early part of the year?

Wind down the river bank

* The last weekend of the year at the cottage.

Sand Martins

AUGUST 20.

D. A splendid sunny day, but windy, and the wind was so cold that it made us feel as if the autumn was come. I did jobs in the garden, fastened sweet-briars across to the fence to make a bank, tied gloire on to the roof, and pegged down some shoots of W.A. Richardson and Rêve d'Or roses, paid the gardener and settled what work wants doing in the winter. We went to our bridge* to say good-bye, and I walked with E. to the end of the lime avenue†. I did not go till 5, feeling softly sad and very tender towards the cottage.

NOVEMBER 17 TO 19.

E. A warm sunny Sunday and nearly quite still. We went a long biscuit walk round Micheldever wood and through the drive across it between tall spruces and large yews, and back by Ashburton's lodge and linnet farm. Thermometer over 50 all day and never fell below 43 at night. Birds singing, especially thrushes: we had luncheon by a singing thrush†† in Micheldever wood, which sang right on all the time: this morning we opened the cottage windows wide to hear them: wrens, robins and larks are the other birds in song, but the thrushes are the most vigorous of all. The travellers' joy is in full beard and catches one's eye from a distance like blackthorn flower in brown hedges. Some fading leaves on oaks, but the woods are brown. There has been plenty of rain lately.

---

* 'Grey's bridge'...that leads into the water-meadows below the cottage.
† Leads from the cottage up to the main Winchester to Itchen Abbas road. A favourite haunt of the Greys' beloved long-tailed tits.
†† Unlike the blackbird, which only sings from March to June, the song thrush recommences his song in the autumn.

1895

MARCH 9 TO JUNE 30

NEAR ALRESFORD

FOG RISING FROM ALRESFORD POND ON A COLD NIGHT. THE POND WAS
ORIGINALLY A RESERVOIR FOR THE VALLEY MILLS. EIGHT HUNDRED YEARS AGO
WINCHESTER WAS ONE OF THE GREAT WOOL MARKETS

MARCH 9 TO 11.

E. There has been a tremendous frost from the latter part of January to the end of February: often below zero: the thermometer in the cottage has apparently been down to 15. We cannot yet say what damage has been done for nothing has begun to grow anywhere yet. The tip of a few lords and ladies* and some snowdrops are the only sign of growing things we saw at all yesterday. But it was a fine day, up to 45, with a S.W. wind and a good deal of sun. We walked to Tichborne, on to Cheriton and home by the downs and the Horseshoe Valley†: rather a mighty round with fine views in places. The air was full of light and there were many innocent white clouds in the sky, which seemed to make the light more, not less. It was the warmest day of the year yet, but without the feeling or smell of spring in it. Few thrushes to be heard: we are afraid the frost has killed many. Tits, chaffinches and hedge sparrows are cheerful enough.

MARCH 11.

> *D.* A most lovely day. I went up wren path and sat on a log in the dry grass watching swans and coots, and when I had sat there about half an hour I heard a chiffchaff just above me in an oak. I wasn't looking out for it at all and I felt as if it might have been singing for just a minute before I heard it. I saw it well through the glasses and heard it twice again. The grass in the withy bed was crackling in the sun and I felt hot air on my face as I walked. There were more thrushes singing than yesterday and some fine resounding nuthatches††. I did not find any long-tailed tits in wren path, they used always to be there. The grass is quite colourless except in water meadows, the great frost has bleached and flattened everything. It is much better to-day than yesterday and still one feels that the spring has not started and there might be frost again in spite of the chiffchaff. I put up a snipe in the oak meadow. Three parters chased each other in the road under the cottage. There is always a fight when three birds get together at this time of year, but pairings seem to get done with very little wrangling on the whole.

Lords and Ladies

* Also known as 'cuckoo-pint'.
† Probably the 'Devil's Punchbowl'. In April 1944, six weeks before D-Day, the US army held a boxing tournament here. It is more recently famous for its crop circles.
†† The springtime 'reeling' song of the nuthatch. Interestingly Grey makes no mention of it in *The Charm of Birds*.

The mill at Itchen Abbas

MARCH 30 AND 31.

E. Pruning Sunday. Disturbed by work* and have to go up on Sunday evening. Cold air, warm sun, rather still, up to 50 in the shade. Buds on sweet-briar, grey-green tufts on honeysuckle, little red points on roses.

Nuthatch

APRIL 6 TO 8.

E. Things look much the same as last Sunday, but there is a more stirring spirit about: we found a chaffinch building in the wren path and heard the first willow wrens and plenty of chiffchaffs. There was a fine rise of trout too. We heard lots of tree-creepers' songs on Sunday. No leaves on hedges or sweet-briar.

* On March 28 1895, Grey as spokesman on Foreign Affairs in the Commons made a pronouncement on Anglo-Egyptian claims to the upper waters of the Nile in view of possible French encroachments. It became known in history as the 'Grey Declaration' and had importance at the time of the Fashoda Incident a few years later.

Blackthorn

MAY 4 TO 6.

E. Cool wind, but bright sun and no stove. Chestnuts are in full leaf and so is the hawthorn: blackthorn in full flower, wild cherry blossom just beginning to fall, sweet-briar leaves very sweet. A hedge sparrow is sitting in our thuja hedge, and a pair of chaffinches building fast in the honeysuckle on the sunny side. D. has found many nests: the chaffinch which was building a month ago in the wren path is sitting: there is a blackcap and sedge warbler with eggs and several hedge sparrows there and in the wild park. There is one long-tailed tit's nest in the wild park too, but the undergrowth there has been all killed by frost and rabbits and the leaves on which the tits must have counted have never come: so the nest is very exposed. Nightingales are plentiful in the usual place and to-day we saw a spotted flycatcher at the cottage, a wood wren singing in the wild park, and a red-backed shrike at the top of the withy bed. The first lots of waterhens' eggs are apparently hatching. Some forward beeches are quite green, others quite brown: elms have enough small leaves to make them look faintly green, but the leaves on the limes are so tiny that the avenues look brown still. D. has found what we think is the very beginning of a nightingale's nest.

MAY 11 TO 13.

E. Two very warm days, up to 69. Saturday was very bright. Sunday was dull grey and the grey day was the warmest. Tea out of doors till 9 o'clock both evenings. Limes are green, chestnuts in flower, oaks green—not so forward as the limes, but forwarder than the limes were last week. What was thought and hoped to be going to be a nightingale's nest is now finished, but it has three whitethroat's eggs in it. The great find however of this week is a cuckoo's egg in a dunnock's nest in the wild park: it is a brown sort of egg not the least like the dunnock's and larger. Close to it is a finished nest, just like the whitethroat's, but so much in the nightingale part that we have faint hopes of finding nightingale's eggs in it, when we come back. It has been glorious to have two such days at this time of year. A pair of garden warblers have been at the cottage all the time, mostly about the chalk pit: the chaffinch on the cottage began to sit this Sunday.

Mr 'Baron' Hunt, a local farmer, drives his carriage through the
ford across the River Dene at Alresford

MAY 13.

D. A splendid day, 74. I sat by the oak tree chalk pit an hour and a half
waiting for kingfishers, but they did not come. Rest of the morning spent in
looking for nightingale nests, found a beginning only. I watched
a cuckoo very close while it was making a lot of noise; it opens
its beak a very little for the first note and shuts it quite up
for the second. Another cuckoo got up from the
ground nearly under my feet but I could see
no nest or egg. I found what looks like a
duck's nest in the wild park, lots of
dark down put in a round place but
no eggs. I am quite prepared for the
nest I think is a nightingale's to turn
into a whitethroat.

MAY 18 AND 19.

E. A cold withering north wind and dull
grey days without sun or shadow. But no
rain fell, which is wanted and the cold seems

Garden Warbler

parching in its dryness. Perhaps the most obstinate wrong-headed weather possible for this time of year and very comfortless. I came late on Friday night the 17th and when I went out before breakfast saw goldfinches getting lichen off the walnut. They flew over the cottage and when I followed I found them and a red-backed shrike sitting on our fence. After breakfast D. found the goldfinches nest close by in one of the limes in the field at the end of a long branch. The hedge sparrow* here which hatched last Monday has had its nest destroyed, but the chaffinch is sitting in all right, and during the week a pair, perhaps *the* pair of spotted flycatchers, have built on the cottage and laid an egg. On Saturday I went up the wren path on my way to fish and found all the nests safe. A chaffinch, a hedge sparrow, two sedge warblers and two blackcaps: on one blackcap nest the hen was sitting, on the other the cock: I saw them both close and neither moved. I believe I have at last found a reed warbler's nest in the reed bed above the withy bed. The garden warblers are here still, but sang very little. On Sunday we went a long walk round by Chilcomb†. Lilac is now at its best: hawthorn is only in tight white buds. Temp. 54 highest, 45 lowest.

MAY 20.

D. The same cold weather, 46. I lit the stove before lunch. Have not succeeded in finding a nightingale nest and felt very low about it. I was sitting on a tree root in a wet place watching wagtails when a stoat put its head out of a hole about two inches off my dress, hissed and made a noise like a loud harsh water-hen several times and then got quiet. I saw a blackbird chase a squirrel about twenty yards along the ground and then attack it as it corkscrewed up a large oak. It hit the squirrel several times. I could not see that the squirrel had an egg in its mouth. Three cuckoos flew about near me by the Aquarium; one of them I am nearly sure had an egg in its mouth and

Stoat

* Also called the dunnock, the name that Grey greatly preferred as described in *The Charm of Birds*.
† A village on the downs south-east of Winchester.

flew down in several places amongst the
long grass, once close to the river. It
was followed and worried by six little
birds. I watched a robin fight. Two
cocks kept at it for a long time and
at last seemed to get their feet locked
together. A very young thrush
evidently thought that something
was being fed, as it came rushing up
to them and opened its mouth at
them as they struggled. They went
away laughing.

Cuckoo and Whitethroat

MAY 25 AND 26.

E. Hawthorn fully out. Chestnuts passing away. Our garden warblers have left
us. I refused to keep the Queen's birthday in London and came here and have
been rewarded by two splendid days, bright and up to 68. We sat out under
the limes all this morning in perfect luxury. The cuckoo's egg has hatched, but
only very lately. The young hedge sparrows are all turned out and the young
cuckoo is a fat naked black thing, which lies sprawling on its stomach. D.
found a nest of nightingales just hatched.

MAY 27.

D. Splendid day, nice breeze, 70. I put a young whitethroat into the nest with
the young cuckoo, which I think is about five days old. On Saturday it was
white and red and to-day it is a sort of blue all over and looks horrid. I put the
whitethroat onto its back and it at once stood up, leaning back with its wings
spread and jerked slightly till it got the little bird onto the edge of the nest. I
caught it and put it back at the bottom of the nest under the cuckoo who
waited for a minute or two looking rather tired. Then it turned on its side and
rubbed the little bird against the side of the nest till it got it squeezed onto its
back, then it waited panting, then it straddled its legs out on each side, butted
its head against the bottom of the nest, spread its wings backward and up and
stood jerking for some time till it got the young bird over the edge, its head
right down all the time. It stood in the same position for quite a long time to
make sure that the bird was really out and then fell down in a heap at the
bottom of the nest quite exhausted. It could not have stood up without using
its head as a lever.

JUNE 7.

E. We came on the 31st of May to stay till June 10, the end of the Whitsuntide holiday. To-day I picked the first moss rose—a gem—and the first gloire de dijon: we had the first basket of strawberries, and the spotted fly-catcher on the cottage hatched. She laid her last egg and began to sit on the 26th May, so that she has hatched in twelve days. She has been constantly on and off the nest and appeared to sit much less steadily than other birds, such as the chaffinch. The young cuckoo in the wild park is dead in the nest, but it has at any rate lived long enough to explain to us how young cuckoos get rid of other little birds from the nest: the great event in bird life for us this year has been the nesting of a pair of red-backed shrikes* in the chalk pit. D. found the nest: there are five eggs and the cock visits the nest occasionally, I suppose to feed the hen. A pair of sparrows† have nested high up in the travellers' joy on the cottage, but the hen will not feed them when I am looking, and does not seem to get any more confidence however still I keep or however long I sit on the bank below. The chaffinch, whose nest was much lower and nearer, soon gained confidence last year and did not mind me. The sparrow, on the other hand, flies to the nest continually, sits about it obtrusively, but won't go in, and keeps eyeing me: a very good instance of the obtrusive familiarity and disagreeable distrust of sparrows. They are the most unlikeable of all birds. A few wild roses were out when we came and have kept coming out since. Our first tea rose, a Souvenir de S.A. Prince, was picked yesterday: it was off a bush which was only bought in the spring, and is said to have been given an unfair start by being grown in a pot. We have had fairly warm bright weather, but a most persistent north wind: everything is very dry: the earth wants rain, and the dry wind seems to be making trees and plants thirsty.

Wild Strawberries

* The red-backed shrike was common and widespread in Britain in the nineteenth century but has declined ever since. 1989 represented the first year in recorded ornithological history when they were not known to have bred in England. The absence of large flying insects is stated as one reason for their decline.
† The house sparrow was the one bird that Grey actively disliked. This is described in the chapter titled 'The Cuckoo and the Sparrow' in *The Charm of Birds*.

JUNE 9 (SUNDAY).
E. The last day of our holiday: it has been bright and
hot, up to 77, and nearly still. We went a walk to
Ovington and above it by the river path in the still
warm evening and fell in with a strange, but
friendly, cat on the furthest bridge above Ovington.
The last songs of birds are to be heard, but the blackbirds are failing fast and the thrushes sing humbly
hidden amongst the dense leaves. All the vigour, almost the
egotism of their spring manner is gone, when they sing by the
hour from a foremost place on a bare tree. Another pair of spotted
flycatchers have come to our garden railing and are doing up the old
nest in which one brood of chaffinches and another of spotted flycatchers were reared last year. The first pair have three young birds,
and the cock, who paid no attention when they were first hatched,
now feeds them constantly. The hen bird often sits on them after
feeding, to cherish them apparently, which seems very thoughtful and touching. Rain is badly wanted. The warm days and hot
sun have made a clump of poppies in our garden come out
passionately. To-night it is so warm that we cannot give up going
out and get to bed. While we were under the limes in the dark a
beautiful little light glowed on Dorothy's arm. We brought it in and
found a little black winged creature.

Poppies

JUNE 15 AND 16.
E. We came by the early train on Saturday and went straight to the
goldfinches' and shrikes' nests—both are all right, but the shrike has not
hatched yet: the young goldfinches are very large and dull about the head.
Wild roses have been at their best for some days apparently: a few stray sweet-
briars are out: elderflower has come. Ragged robin, forget-me-not, and yellow
iris, still all over the water-meadows as they have been for a long time. Very
pleasant days, up to 62 and 66, and bright, but very cold nights, 36 and 38.
Plenty of our roses of all kinds are out, but only one white moss, though there
are any number of gem and several of the common kind. The honeysuckle is
very good and pretty and strong. The songs of birds are scarce, the ripple of a
blackcap's notes is as frequent as any. The old nest which was being done up by
the spotted flycatchers has been undone, probably by sparrows, which are
building near.

Itchen Abbas station: a small station on a branch line, yet with five permanent staff

JUNE 22 AND 23.

E. Warm days, up to 76 on Sunday and fine with a south breeze. The singing of birds is nearly over: a thrush sang near the cottage clearly and quietly this afternoon, but we have no wren singing in the chalk pit as there was this time last year: perhaps it likes to keep away from the shrikes. The shrikes have hatched and the young ones have heads like pterodactyls. The flycatchers on the cottage and the goldfinches have fledged safely: there has been a very successful brood of coots in the cottage meadow and bird events are over for this season. The honeysuckle is glorious and there are dense masses of flowers on the sunny side of the cottage, where the aphis has destroyed it all every year before. There are plenty of wild roses and our sweet-briar is fairly in flower. The Ayrshire rose has one or two flowers only, but the big blow of the rose beds seems to have come. We

Sweet-briar

had two very fine Archduchesses and more La Frances and Gloire de Dijons than were wanted for our cottage room, and Captain Christies too. The white mosses are not out yet; they were first in 1893, second to the gem last year, and the latest of all three now. Still no rain: the drought has not lasted so long as in 1893, but with that exception I think it is as severe as any I remember: the glass is very high and all prospect of rain seems far away. We watered the tea roses well both last Sunday and this. The Government were beaten on Friday night, and we have spent these days in high hopes of an announcement on Monday, which will bring the end of this terrible time* within sight.

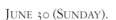

Red-backed Shrike

JUNE 30 (SUNDAY).

E. I came on Thursday afternoon: the Government have resigned. I shall never be in office again and the days of my stay in the House of Commons are probably numbered. We are both very glad and relieved, but there has come to us an unexpected sadness on account of our cottage. The freedom for which we have longed is coming, but it will take us away from this place†, and it is as if in wishing for the thing that has come we had been all the time thoughtlessly lapsing into disloyalty to our cottage: ungrateful to it we have never been not even for a moment. However, of the future it seems as if we should now be able to say that whatever is to be will be best, and things shall take a natural course without sharp corners. Meanwhile we go north for the election this week, and have taken long leave of the cottage and Itchen.

On Friday the drought gave way and there came a good rain, some twelve hours of it, not very heavy but soaking. The birds seem to have sung a little more since, chiefly thrushes and blackbirds. There is a cottage chiff-chaff this year instead of a cottage wren, and numbers of goldfinches come

---

* From 1892 to 1895 Grey had been in office as Under-Secretary of State for Foreign Affairs and during this time an interest and pleasure in country things had been taking a stronger hold of him. He had become increasingly miserable at the tie to London and the curtailment of his time in the country.

† Grey means they will have to go north to live at Fallodon.

and go about us. A sandpiper* is in the cottage meadows to-day, and we heard a grasshopper warbler† this evening from our rose beds. The young shrikes got out of the nest yesterday afternoon, but they are hidden in a thicket and we only know where they are by the excitement of the old birds, who go about with food in their mouths including what looks like raw pieces of little bird: but we cannot find any larder††. The Lonicera is fully out, and there is still a bigger blow of roses than last week. Honeysuckle and sweet-briar are at their best. The Ayrshire rose not come to it yet.

Common Sandpiper

* This could either be a common (most likely) or a green sandpiper. It would be early for either to be moving south from their nesting grounds. Today green sandpipers winter in the Itchen valley and frequent the local cressbeds.
† A shy summer migrant that spends its time feeding in dense cover. Grey likens its song in *The Charm of Birds* to 'a small soft running reel'. As the evenings get warmer it becomes a night-time singer.
†† Red-backed shrikes have a gruesome habit of impaling their prey on thorns for storage purposes.

1896

MARCH 7 TO JULY 13

ALRESFORD POND

A VIEW FROM THE ALTON TO WINCHESTER RAILWAY LINE. WHEN THE POND WAS
FIRST DAMMED IT COVERED ABOUT TWO HUNDRED ACRES

Treecreeper

MARCH 7 TO 9.

E. We came on Saturday morning: it is more than eight months since we were here, but hardly anything has changed: there is one new gate near us and a new fastening on another one and a new bridge in the water meadows: that is about all. But changes have happened to us: I am out of office*, though not free of politics: and we have learnt to ride bicycles† and brought them with us meaning to get out at Alton and ride them here: a reckless and hard-hearted innovation, which was stopped by the weather. We were prepared to rush into this dear place on bicycles for the first time in a way, which I now see was inconsiderate and wanting in reverence to a place which has kept itself so unchanged for us. The rain obliged us to come by train in the usual way and to walk the bicycles humbly and thoughtfully down: they have remained unused since, and out of sight, and great as is the part they will play in our times here, they will begin slowly.

The winter has been a complete contrast to the one before it. There has been no snow and hardly any frost, not one day's skating anywhere; but last year's rainfall was deficient, January was below the average and February was exceptionally dry. So our only grudge against the wet weather now is that much of the rain has been drizzle only. These two days have been soft in every way: soft in temperature, soft in rain, soft grey in colour, making everything soft in outline and sometimes veiled in fine rain. Missel thrushes, blackbirds, thrushes, wrens, larks, and robins are singing well: chaffinches are frequent but unfinished: yellowhammers are not sure of their cheese: we heard a treecreeper and a golden-crested wren††, at any rate one of them certainly, and kingfishers, I am glad to say, more than once. A thrush has built in the alcove of the cottage and is sitting on four eggs. Honeysuckle has tufts of grey-green leaves, roses

* Lord Salisbury is now Prime Minister and the Liberals will remain in opposition for a decade. Grey was in fact returned to Parliament by his constituents with an increased majority.
† Became an important part of the Greys' lives at the cottage, especially on Sundays when there was no fishing.
†† In *The Charm of Birds*, in the chapter titled 'Increasing Song', Grey tells us how as a young man he used to confuse the high-pitched songs of the treecreeper and goldcrest. In the wild park at Avington there are many evergreens, a favourite haunt of the goldcrest. Grey tells us that the goldcrest's call-notes are 'like needle-points of sound', and the song suggests 'a tiny stream trickling and rippling over a small pebbly channel, and at the end going over a miniature cascade'.

The sexton cuts the grass with a scythe in Twyford churchyard

have little shoots as well as points and plenty of last year's leaves: the sweet-briar has shoots all over and some tiny leaves. D. found a few white violets out and the elm trees are in full flower. Temp. 52 and 43.

MARCH 14 TO 16.
E. I bicycled from Alton in the middle of the day: afterwards D. and I went to Winchester and brought back a dozen tea roses. It was a warm evening and we sat on the bridge here, with our feet hanging over the water, listening to the birds till nearly seven o'clock. The thrush has four young birds some days old, so she must have laid in February: both old birds feed the young ones. Sunday was windy and not so nice a day: temp. 28 and 47. White violets are out, and the pale patch in the garden is in full flower.

MARCH 21 TO 23.
E. There had been heavy rain in the week; every-thing was soft and soaked when we came at midday on Saturday. It was mild enough, and there was more stir

White Violets

than ever amongst birds and things. Two pairs of goldfinches, if not more, were singing and twittering close to the cottage all day: we picked a mass of white violets in the oak meadow. Sunday has been wonderful, hot and bright till well in the afternoon. I walked over the downs, by Telegraph, to Morestead and Shawford. Chiffchaffs are common. I saw two wheatears near the horseshoe valley, just where we saw the first wheatear once before, and not another anywhere in all my walking: the larks were glorious on the high open ground, and in the valleys the air was rich with the sound of blackbirds. I sat under the great yew by Twyford church* and listened to the organ in the church: in the evening the thrushes round the cottage sang till seven o'clock. D. went different ways and heard a willow wren: there have been some sounds like a blackcap or garden warbler, but rather faint and seldom and always followed by much robin song[†]: we have had slight differences of opinion about these. Young thrushes nearly fledged: chaffinches thought to be building on cottage. Thermometer 50 at 5 p.m., must have been higher in day.

APRIL 24 TO 27.

E. We came on Friday and made much of our time. It has been a fine warm spring, but April has been too dry, and there is still no prospect of rain. Chestnut leaves are out and the flower is beginning, blackthorn fading: beech woods are brown but with patches of green in them: limes cannot be called green at all yet, but some young oaks are in the small yellow stage. The country is very pretty, the trees which are green are so fresh and bright and show up with such a happy spirit against those which are bare and brown. A tree in fresh new leaf is like something surprised by a great joy: it catches your eye and

Wheatear

* I sat under the great yew at Twyford church myself on March 20 1998. It is over three hundred years old and surrounded by a wooden seat. Twyford is south-east of Winchester and would have represented a long hard walk from the cottage, demonstrating Grey's general athleticism.
[†] Mid March would be too early to hear a blackcap or garden warbler. In his chapter 'Early Song', in *The Charm of Birds*, Grey writes, 'In April, when thoughts are turned to summer warblers, I have even heard one or two notes in a robin's song that prompt the exclamation, "blackcap"!'

asks you to share it. All orchards are in flower. On Saturday we bicycled to Alton through Chawton wood: the trees of the wood were on the whole brown, but there were many flowers and we heard a nightingale on the way to it. All song-birds have come, but there is no willow wren* near the cottage yet. Our thrush has hatched a second brood in the same nest: a chaffinch and green-finch are building in the chalk pit: we suspect the kingfishers of having a nest in the old upturned willow, and a wren is sitting on eggs behind the ivy which hangs from its prostrate stem. Sunday was a good day: a light warm breeze from the west, a good deal of sun, and the air bright always. We went by train to Salisbury and bicycled back†, getting foundered and lost in the old Roman road, but finding our way back to the Stockbridge road after much walking and many miles. It was more than I could take in—the town, the cathedral, the great country over which we came, the many

Horse Chestnut flower

places, which we passed, pressing on because we were so late, and the light, which we saw looking back towards the evening sun from the tops of hills.

A willow wren has come to the chalk pit since I wrote last night. Swifts have been seen. Lowest temp. 39, 49, and 38. Highest on Saturday 57. On Sunday the sun shone on the thermometer: it went up to 65.

MAY 1 TO 5.

E. Friday to Tuesday broken by a visit of one night to Netley. The 2nd of May was bitter: cold wind and no sun. Temp. fell to 26 and never rose above 49. The two day temperatures have been 49 and 55: the nights 26, 33, 32, 30. What harm the frost has done we cannot yet tell, but the chief thing of this visit has been *Frost*. The thrush on the cottage took her second brood off on the 3rd. A chaffinch is building and laying as it builds close to our big window through which we go in and out. The kingfishers have a nest in the old willow: I saw the bird go out, and waded round to look at the opening. I waited, but though kingfishers came about they brought no food and there were no signs of young.

---

* More commonly known as the willow warbler. Their absence is surprising; with a warm spring as stated, they should have arrived by April 1.
† Again demonstrating Grey's athletic nature.

*Ploughing with oxen had almost died out by the turn of the century but was
still carried on at Mr Waterman's farm at Selborne*

MAY 7 TO 12.

E. Strong north-east wind and hardly a cloud all these days: the power of per-
petual sun has warmed the air steadily: the thermometer got
up to 69 to-day (11th), and yesterday we left off our light-
ing the stove and began to sit out after sunset. Everything
is green except ashes, walnuts, the tall poplars and a
few very old oaks. Hawthorn* is out everywhere, but
not quite at the full: lilac plentiful. We have found
several chaffinches' nests in the wren path and one
bullfinch, but no warblers yet. Yesterday D. found a
bumble bee stuck on a blackthorn, and to-day we saw a
shrike near it: we hope it is on its way to the nest in the
chalk pit again. We have taken great delight in the
singing of one special blackbird close to the cottage: he has
wonderful cadences in his song. On Sunday I bicycled over to

Peonies

* Grey wrote to his friend Captain Barton, 'I love the smell of the hawthorn, but it is very nearly a
nasty smell, and it is now clear to me that the hawthorn, being in nature pure and innocent and
full of good intentions, has all but stumbled into a horrible mistake and made a mess of its smell.'

Middleton: the Watneys are leaving it, and this was their
last day there: I, too, wanted to take leave of it, for
I have had some kind days there and have seen
them looking at their roses and loving the
place. The frost has nipped many young
shoots and killed all the tiny acacia leaves,
and I have not quite been able to enjoy
the glory of these days for thinking of
the want of rain. We are still denied
even the promise or hope of it.

MAY 15 TO 18.
E. Came in the dark on Friday. Still
no promise of rain, and the mown
grass is turning brown, but with that
exception the face of everything is so fair
that one cannot believe there is any hidden
want. Everything is green except ashes and

Swifts

walnuts: our old walnut here had its leaves killed by
the frost and has all its start to do over again like the acacias. Warm days, up to
65 and not below 52 last night, but no sun till to-day, which is bright and
promises to be really hot. A few china roses are just out, and two peonies are
glowing in the garden. The shrikes *are* in the chalk pit: I saw them first thing on
Saturday morning, and found a new but empty nest, on which, however, the
female shrike is now sitting. I saw the male bird feed her when she was not on
the nest but in a bush yesterday.

We bicycled over to Selborne on Sunday and came back by East Tisted,
Bramdean, Cheriton, etc. Selborne is a dull village, but the hanging wood and
the high common look interesting. Perhaps one can write best living in a dull
place with nothing to distract one's attention, but with many opportunities for
seeing things in places near. We sat under the tree outside the vicarage and
churchyard and looked at the oldest cottages as some which the little man*
might have been in and out of and listened to the swifts skirling round: there
are said to be the same number of pairs as he counted.

A little bird with a monotonous and rapid note has plagued me all these
days: I have spent hours sitting opposite or under it without ever getting a

* Gilbert White, famous for *The Natural History of Selborne*.

Lesser Whitethroat

really good sight of it, but I think it is a lesser whitethroat*. It was often feeding among the young oak leaves, and kept "gabbling" its song, but I could not catch sight of it. All sorts of other birds would come and show themselves to me, close to it, but the "gabbling" noise went on unseen. The shrike has eggs of the same pattern as last year.

JUNE 12 TO 15.

E. We have been away at Fallodon and Littlecote†, but came at last by the early train on Friday morning. There has been rain but only quite lately. The Itchen Abbas children—at least I suppose it is some of them—have searched the chalk pit mercilessly and pulled out all the nests I know of including the shrike's, but I still see the birds about and the hen has a meditative air and visits bushes and sits thinking as if she was planning another nest. The spotted flycatchers have built again a few inches above the old place, which they had last year.

Wild roses are gay, but almost past their best and we are only just in time for the big blow of honeysuckle. Lonicera is coming out fast and so is sweet-briar and the Ayrshire rose, which all have many flowers. Our garden roses are just beginning. The days have been very warm, up to 75, and the nights warm too, and in the dusk our room and the lawn are full of the smell of honeysuckle. Elderflower too is out. To-day (Sunday) I have been on a long bicycle ride to Stockbridge††, thence to Houghton and back by King's Somborne and Sparsholt. It was bright and hot, but the air was very hazy and one feels that spring is far behind and it is full summer. The beeches are all dark and look almost stiff with sturdy beech nuts, when one is close to them. The hawthorn is all a dull colour and instead of its bright blossom there are clusters of unrejoicing berries, which seem to think nothing of the suns of spring, which helped to make them, and will need many summer suns to make them colour. The elderflower honours the season in a stiff practical way,

---

* A far-carrying, rattling song given within deep cover. This recognition proves Grey has already become a top-flight ornithologist.
† The home of the Watney family near Hungerford; now a hotel.
†† On the River Test.

but the sprays of wild roses are perfect in joy, I saw a wonderful sight of poppies in a recess in a wheat field, where the wheat was thin: they seemed to make the day hotter, but I was bold and liked the heat. I left my glasses at Stockbridge and did not find it out till I was more than half way home: and it took six miles each way of the stones and hills of the Stockbridge road to go to fetch them, but I was rewarded, for just as the extra miles were done and I was once again on my way home, I heard a poor, but new song and saw the bird on the top of a yew tree in the hedge. It was a real cirl bunting*, the first I have ever seen, and it sang several times and I had a good look at it. It seemed rather suspicious of me, and without the glasses, though I might have suspected it, I could never have made sure.

JUNE 27.

E. D. has been here since the 19th and I several days since then. Charlie† came for two days this week and enjoyed the fishing and liked the place. We have had ordinary summer weather, not above 70, but very pleasant. Plenty of roses have been in flower all the time and for the last week the Ayrshire rose and privet have been having their season. The songs of birds are ceasing gradually: there come little wisps of sweet blackbird song out of thick leaves now and then, sometimes with an almost pensive cadence. We have noticed the quality and cadences of blackbirds' notes particularly this year. To-day a blackcap came to the chalk pit and sang all day, as it did at this season about two years ago. I think a shrike is sitting in the chalk pit again, but the nest is too high up for me to be sure of the bird: I found a field mouse one day stuck upon a thorn, and partly eaten, in thick bushes on the slope of the chalk. I found two reed warblers' nests up the river, and see several young ones about: to-day in my fishing I came upon young reed warblers, young pheasants, a brood of little wild ducks and one of tiny partridges. A

Elderflower

* There is a delightful description of Grey's first encounter with a cirl bunting in *The Charm of Birds* in the chapter titled 'From Full to Least Song'. Since the time of writing the cirl has declined drastically in numbers across southern England primarily due to changes in farming practices, notably the absence of winter stubbles for foraging.
† Edward Grey's brother, who was killed by a buffalo in Africa in 1928.

strange thing has happened to the thrushes' nest on the cottage, from which two broods have been fledged this season—a pair of pied wagtails have built in it: they are very tame and had amused us by their antics and flirtations in front of us on the lawn for several days before we found their nest. Both D. and I have often gone in search of wagtails' nests and never found one—now they have come to us.

Common Privet

JULY 4 TO 6.

E. A very short time: I did not get down till Saturday evening. Sunday was a brilliant day, up to 72 and not a cloud. A big blow of roses still goes on, but a lot of things are over. Lime flower is well out and we sat under it a great deal: a family of great tits were with us nearly all the time, but very few birds sing at all and one listens to the hum of bees and feels that it is the very height of midsummer. In the afternoon we went to the tame park* and found the water-lilies well grown and out: a charm of goldfinches were in the trees above and three of them flew low over the water, with the sun on their colours, and there was much twittering and singing. I can see nothing of the shrikes and must have been mistaken as to their second nest. The honeysuckle on the east side of the cottage has come into very fine bloom a second time.

JULY 8 TO 13 (WEDNESDAY TO MONDAY).

E. The last days—warm with a hot Sunday and plenty of sun to end with in which we bicycled to Stockbridge and came back by Houghton, etc. Wagtails and flycatchers on the cottage fledged. Rain is badly wanted and the roses are perishing for want of it. Another Itchen season is over and once more we are going away, full of gratitude and a sense that the spring and summer have not been wasted upon us. A few fields of corn have been cut and the glory of trees and flowers is past, but the sense of the bounty and luxury of summer is everywhere: one feels caressed by it and, though there is less regret in our leave-taking than if the best of the south were not over, it is very tender.

* Mature parkland to the west of Avington Park.

1897

MAY 16 TO JULY 18

NEAR AVINGTON

THE WINDING COURSE OF THE ITCHEN BEFORE IT REACHES ITCHEN ABBAS. THE
TREES ON THE LEFT MARK THE BEGINNING OF AVINGTON PARK

MAY 16.

E. We came on the 13th. Many things have happened since we were last here: we spent the early months of this year in the West Indies* and did not come back to England till May, but now we are at the cottage again feeling great joy, because everything is so nice and so known. The spring is cold and rather late: there has been frost, which has completely killed the first green efforts of ashes, walnuts and acacia, but the limes and beeches are very fresh and green; oaks are showing colour freely: lilac is just out, hawthorn beginning to show in some places, but mostly only in bud. For once there has been no spring drought and the river is fuller than it has been for several years. A gale has blown down many trees since we were last here, but none near the cottage. A lime in the big avenue and some of the immemorial elms near it are gone: they were great elms and well known. But the worst change is that our "Hiddin" has been cut down: the bushes may grow up again, but the tall willows we shall never see any more: they were the first green trees in spring and in April I have heard them full of the hum of bees.

A blackbird and a thrush have hatched on the cottage: a chaffinch has built in the porch and laid three eggs, but seems to have disliked our coming and has deserted. A nest, believed to be a lesser whitethroat's is in the chalk pit: the bird is sitting on eggs, but leaves the nest whenever we pass near and is difficult to see.

To-day I went a bicycle to Stockbridge and up the Test to Wherwell and back by the long line of beeches. At one place I saw a lot of beeches whose young leaves had been completely killed by frost and the trees looked terribly brown and bare. But all else was bright and beautiful and I lay for some time under the green of young beech leaves reading. It hasn't been warm: thermometer down to 31 and only on one day up to 62, on other days it didn't reach 60.

MAY 17.

D. E. having gone up to London I have spoken no word all day except "dinner at half past five please Susan†." The wagtails have been fiddling with the old thrush's nest but don't seem serious. Up wren

Acacia

* In 1897 Grey joined a Royal Commission to inquire into the economic difficulties of the British West Indies; one of the very few overseas trips he ever made. The Commission pointed out the dangers of over-reliance on sugar and suggested various remedies.
† Susan Drover was their local housekeeper at the cottage.

Children from Avington village school dance around the maypole in Avington Park

path I found two chaffinch, one parter, one sedge, and six wren nests, of which the last three were cock* nests, one lined but empty, one with one egg, and one with young. There were many wrens to be seen and I watched two who were climbing up trees and going along branches and taking notice of each other all the time. I felt very loving towards them, and when I began to read again I did not like the book, Keats' love letters. Keats and Fanny Brawn† don't compare well with wrens. We have never had such a complete set of wrens nests before. Sitting by jaw hatches after sunset and getting sort of deaf with the noise, it was nice coming away and hearing all the evening singing again, an interval makes it seem more wonderful. I found a hole in a rotten branch in wren path just the right size for a lesser spotted††, but it is too low down to be real I'm afraid. It is new

Wren's nest

* The cock wren builds a number of nests as part of the courtship process.
† Dorothy's wrens would have enjoyed a natural cosy, conjugal relationship unlike Keats and Fanny. His letters to her are obsessive, imploring, passionate, intense and hysterical.
†† The lesser-spotted woodpecker is small, about the size of a chaffinch and tends to frequent the high canopy and is therefore not as accessible as the greater-spotted.

Avington house from across the lake in the park

though and has certainly been made by a woodpecker. We shall see! There has been much wind all day and the young lime leaves double up so under it that it seems cruel. In the afternoon it got warm suddenly, and I have been sitting on our bridge in the dark with the river so high that it touches the bridge and makes an odd noise.

Lesser-spotted Woodpecker

MAY 23.

E. I have been up and down. There has been a steady cold wind, but very bright cloudless days and we have had our tea out of doors twice and foregone the stove in the evening. Spotted flycatchers have come to the cottage and look at it as if parts were familiar to them, but I doubt if any will nest on it while we are here. The wagtails carry on with the old thrush's nest, in which they reared a brood last year, but our being about makes them unsettled too. We are beginning to want rain.

MAY 23.

E. I went in my waders to examine the kingfisher's place: one of them flew out close to me and I found one of the holes very dirty and could hear the young birds inside very distinctly. A pair of bluetits are carrying the moss away from the blackbird's nest on the cottage to the top of one of the poplars. I watched them as I was sitting out, and saw the spotted flycatchers going to what I believe they have chosen for a nest, and a queen wasp getting wood off the trellis for her nest: it was the noise of the wasp sawing the wood that first made me notice her.

Queen Wasp

JUNE 3.

E. We are going to Littlecote for some days. I was here on the 30th and 31st: but it was cold and we had the stove. On Sunday afternoon a female bunting was in the poplars which seemed to me unfamiliar, and soon afterwards I was looking through the glasses at a fine male cirl bunting. He passed on and I haven't heard his song or had time to go about watching for him. It has become fairly warm at last: there has been plenty of rain and the young lesser whitethroats are nearly ready to fly. A young robin became tame and came indoors: D. fed it with raw meat as it sat on my head but it was rather stupid.

I have found a cuckoo's egg in a reed warbler's nest just above the wagon bridge.

JUNE 15.

E. We are here again. Wild roses are fully out: sweet-briar showing freely and the chalk pit is sturdy with elderflower. Very cool weather and no roses out except one W.A. Richardson on the cottage.

JUNE 21.

E. For six days the thermometer hasn't reached 60, and it has been down to 42 and 45. Our first white moss rose was picked yesterday and the first tea rose, a Safrano, and the first La France to-day. There have been several gem moss roses and to-day we have the beginning of a rose table.

I went to see how the cuckoo's egg had done in the reed warbler's nest and found a very repulsive red-gaping, ill-tempered cuckoo alone in the nest stretching it. Hardly any birds sing, except wrens: I have heard very few chiff-chaffs and willow wrens here this year.

To-day is warmer and will bring flowers on: the earth is moist with rains.

JUNE 22.

D. Up wren path on 17th I found a new cock nest, and out of it came a stream of strong young wrens. On the 19th, about the same time of day, 7 o'clock, they were in again. They must go in there to sleep. The stopping of the singing of thrushes and blackbirds seems to make room for other little songs. I have heard more willow wrens, chiffchaffs and larks to-day than for some time. Found a yellowhammer nest with young in oak meadow*.

JUNE 27 (SUNDAY).

E. This last week may be called the week of the honeysuckle and sweet-briar. Sweet-briar is now at its best: the honeysuckle is dropping fast and the Lonicera flowering hard. The Ayrshire rose began to flower on the 25th. We had two hot days in the week, up to 75 and 77, which brought everything on. For the last few days we have had plenty of roses. Privet is out.

I went a walk this afternoon—a round so well known that I went it mostly for the pleasure of its memories—up the road past Itchen wood, along the end of Micheldever wood, up to Ashburton's Lodge, and so back by Itchen down and Linnet Farm. But I saw new things. It was a dull, misty afternoon, damp and heavy, and as I looked over Avington Parks from the opposite side they looked dim and brown as if it was not summer: but a few hazy gleams of light lit up spots of bright green, which looked like spring coming amongst

Yellowhammer

* Directly behind the cottage.

Village children in Avington Park

the brown. I was alone, not a soul in sight, and it was as if I was looking on and seeing nature dreaming of the spring that is past. The long piece of grass beyond Itchen wood was covered with lady's slipper: I never saw such a mass of it: it made the whole length glow, and as I walked through it the scent rose up all round me: it was full of bees and quantities of ripe red wild strawberries were dotted about, and patches of beautiful blue burrage stood up here and there. Was there ever such a gay place before? with a male red-backed shrike, too, sitting in the hedge beside it all.

Wild Strawberries

JULY 5.

E. The Ayrshire rose is in full bloom: only some top honey-suckle flowers are left: the Lonicera is proceeding steadily to the tips of each spray and has nearly reached them. Sweet-briar is practically over: elder is over: privet has been out for a week: and two days ago the limes had enough flowers open to attract bees. But there have been cool days lately and windy. A blackcap has been about the cottage for a week singing the whole day through, as it did once before about this time.

JULY 18

E. The last day of our long time here has come. D. goes to Fallodon to-morrow, and I leave too, but expect to be here later on again for a day or two.

Everything has been very quiet: old birds are mostly in the moult and young ones are spreading about and discovering the world for themselves. The river and lakes are full of broods of waterhens, coots, dabchicks and ducks: at least three broods of tufted ducks* belong to the wild park lake. The young cuckoo in the reed bed was destroyed by some vermin, for I found its feathers: but another cuckoo's egg just like the first was laid in a new reed warbler's nest this month and is now a solitary young bird in the nest growing feathers. I saw a fine brood of shrikes yesterday on the down bank above the withy bed, and last Sunday I passed a wryneck on a rail within five yards: I was bicycling slowly and had a good look.

Lime flower, Lonicera, and the Ayrshire rose are all just at their end, though they began on very different dates. We have had plenty of roses and some hot days this week, up to 78. There has been no rain this month and our lawn is getting brown.

E. I was at the cottage again twice for two days: once with V. J. W†. and once with E. Tennant†† early in August. But things had failed because of the dry weather: the roses were limp and poor, and the hedges and trees looked tired. The country too did not smell very fresh.

Wryneck

---

* First reported breeding in Britain in 1849. Resident numbers have increased dramatically in the last fifty years with the increase in gravel pits. There is a substantial influx of European birds in the winter. They were prolific breeders on Avington lake 100 years ago.
† Vernon Watney.
†† Husband of Grey's second wife, Pamela; he became Lord Glenconner in 1910.

1898

MARCH 5 TO JULY 10

AVINGTON PARK

VIEW FROM THE BRIDGE THAT CARRIES THE ITCHEN ABBAS ROAD. AVINGTON
PARK WAS THE HOME OF LORD NORTHBROOK, SIR EDWARD GREY'S COUSIN

MARCH 5 TO 8 (SATURDAY TO TUESDAY).

E. Things are very forward after an extremely mild winter. There are tufts of leaves on the honeysuckle and little green points are opening on the sweet-briar. The roses have been very rash and Laurette Messinny and Rêve d'Or are covered with new shoots. It has been very cold on these days, 23 and 39 were the extremes on Sunday in the shade, and Monday wasn't much better: there has been a cold wind and often a dull sky, but sometimes the sun shone hot on a sheltered bank and from the cottage we could see the rippling stream below the cottage bridge running in the brightness. We found two white violets (one each) in the oak meadow, and the beginning of a thrush's (?) nest in the wren path and were very pleased to be here. We pruned the creepers.

MARCH 18 TO 21 (FRIDAY TO MONDAY).

E. A very nice contrast of days: the first one dull and mild, over 50 and not below 45. After that the wind went to the north, but was gentle: we had bright warm sun all day and 8 degrees of frost at night. I went a long walk on Sunday to Shawford over the downs, in the sun, under the larks, and by the river. Violets are out: there are four sorts: pale blue, pale violet (English we call it), fine purple, and white. All the last three smell very sweet, but the purple kind is very rare. A man has cut down the straggling hedge and some of the ivy, where the stock-doves used to come in front of the cottage. This is sad: and there is a new line of telephone posts right down the water meadows in our special meadow wandering place*. The people here are mad upon telephones: there is another line by the withy bed. All these changes are to the bad and there are always some every winter.

The birds have been singing well, but we have not heard a chiffchaff yet. Blackbirds are in song as well as the rest: there are kingfishers haunting the old willow root: the pair were flying about close to the cottage on Saturday and I saw both their fiery breasts

Blue Violets

* The water-meadows directly across the river from the cottage. A line of telephone posts still runs across the meadow.

together in a bush in the sun. D. found
long-tailed tits building in the larch
plantation and we watched them at
work—high-peering as usual. One
willow bush in the hedge shows green
against the view of the cottage from the
meadows by Chilland.

Long-tailed Tit's nest

APRIL 2 TO 4.
D. I came down earlier than E. and visited the
long-tails. The nest is roofed but feels flimsy as if
it was not lined. Lots of white violets amongst the
ivy in the larch wood. There is a thrush and a blacker*
nest on the cottage, and a moss beginning. The old nest under
pent-house is all pulled about. On Sunday 6 I pollarded the
acacias and we both pruned roses, leaving the newly planted. Up wren path†
found a large bed of dark sweet violets and while we were picking them, long-
tails came above and were watched to their nest high up in an ash fork. We
could only just see that they were high-peering all right. I watched another
pair into the tussock place other side of the shallows, but they were idle and
did not build and could not be found. One thrush egg and one blacker on a
nest were found. The swans were sitting together on their nest; leaning far over
and pulling mud and leaves and stuff into it: a great deal of neck work. The
first chiffchaff was heard by hiddin while the acacias were pollarded. I heard
kinglets†† once but they rather bring a pang because of the traps.

E. We were prevented from coming last week by bitter gales and frost and
snow. There isn't much change this time, except the chiffchaffs. The volume of
song is much greater and wakes us in the early morning, and the air is made
richer now by the songs of blackbirds, which makes the missel thrushes sound
harsh and thin. It was rather a nice April Sunday, 50 and 42.

---

* Blackbird.
† I walked down wren path 100 years later on April 23 1998 – a lovely spring morning with the
cherry blossom in bloom. The long-tailed tits were present, as were wrens, chaffinches, goldcrests
and willow warblers, all of whom were in full song. I saw the first swallow and heard the first
blackcap of the year. The only surprise for the Greys would have been several pairs of gadwall on
the shallows at the end of Avington lake; a dabbling duck that has increased its range
substantially over the past century.
†† I imagine the waterkeeper had set traps for the kingfishers.

The village band leads Avington's May Queen through Avington Park

APRIL 30 TO MAY 4 (SATURDAY TO WEDNESDAY).

E. We came late on the 30th and the 1st of May was gloomy, cold and wet. Temp. 49 and 36. We don't grudge the rain and are glad that the earth is moist. It isn't an early spring now: the limes are quite brown, the wild park brown too: a few beeches are green elsewhere: beeches are never unanimous about the season and here and there one will be well in leaf, while the rest near it are strictly bare. Hawthorn and chestnuts are green, but otherwise there is very little change in the look of things since we were here a month ago.

MAY 7 TO 10 (SATURDAY TO TUESDAY).

E. Damp and cool on Sunday, but a fine bright May day on Monday: up to 64, no stove, early dinner, late tea and evening with windows open. Lime avenue brown still, even the oaks are gaining on it. Beeches are out, that is the main advance, and their new leaves with the sun on them made the tame park smile. We have found several dunnocks' nests, one with a cuckoo's egg of the brown type as usual. Spotted flycatchers have come. There are good nightingales up by the little larch wood: we know of three robin nests and of one lot of young besides, which are fledged, in the chalk pit. Both this time and last

Dunnock's egg

the smell of sweet-briar has been very active: this is its most fragrant stage.

MAY 13 TO 17 (FRIDAY TO TUESDAY).
E. Very cold when we came on Friday evening, and a wet night followed, but after that we had a beautiful day steadily warmed by the sun and ending with tea out of doors at night. I call this book to witness that this is the latest spring of which it has any record. To-day, the 14th, the big lime avenue* is bare and brown, our lime avenue is only spotty green, the cottage poplars are leafless, and there

Blue Tit

is neither lilac, hawthorn, nor chestnut flower. D. has found, what we feel must be a new nightingale nest in the larch copse, but it is still empty. The lesser whitethroat is in the chalk pit again and has five eggs: a blackbird's nest there, which only fledged this week, has now two fresh eggs. A blue tit is building in the cottage roof: it carries up large bunches with great efforts, and its male sits about idly and won't help.

MAY 16.
E. I have seen chestnut flowers and lilac, but only a little: they are not general and there isn't a bit of hawthorn. The beeches are very luxuriant, tender and beautiful. Still no shade in the limes. There have been falls of rain, especially at night, the earth is very moist and we are safe from drought for this month. The nightingale's nest has two eggs.

MAY 25 TO JUNE 2.
E. We came yesterday for Whitsuntide. It has been cold, but the limes really are in leaf, though not thick yet. Chestnut, lilac, and hawthorn are fairly out. Oaks in small leaf and walnut very small. Lesser whitethroat's nest destroyed: several new blackbirds and thrushes—nightingale sitting on five eggs. The grass is very lush and abundant, even in the old cottage field, where we have so often seen it wispy and dry and dusty. River very low from want of winter rain, but we have never escaped drought in April and May completely.

* Running parallel to the Itchen east of Avington Park (*see* page 107).

Swallow

JUNE 6.

E. We had a mild evening and morning on Saturday and Sunday. On Sunday I went on a bicycle ride—round by Middleton, Wherwell and Stockbridge. The air was very sweet. But with that exception it has been very cold and stormy with a cruel N.W. wind, which has broken boughs with leaves and tender rose shoots. Temperature fell to 40 last night and has only reached 52 to-day. The birds are quite disheartened and hardly sing at all. The nightingale's nest has been destroyed, which has grieved us. It is still chestnut, lilac and hawthorn time. The limes are a pretty green, but their foliage is not really thick yet, and the old walnut has only very small red leaves. A pair of swallows have built in our porch and are beginning to sit on five eggs.

JUNE 23.

E. We came back on the 17th, D. to stay and I to be here as much as I can. Wild roses were out when we came and the elderflower. The sweet-briar and honeysuckle are just beginning to show now. Only two roses have yet been picked. Till the 17th there had been hardly anything but cold weather; we just came here in time for some warm days of fair summer weather, but we haven't had the thermometer once up to 70 yet. There is a cuckoo's egg in a sedge warbler's nest in the chalk pit: there is no other egg in the nest and the sedge warbler is sitting very closely, so I suppose the other eggs have been removed by the old cuckoos, though I have not seen an instance of this before. D. has found a shrike's nest in the withy bed: there has been a brood of young shrikes there often. I went a long bicycle ride on Sunday, by Tichborne, Cheriton, Bramdean, West Meon, Wansford, and back over the high down by Kilmeston: it was fine and warm and smelling of new-mown hay.

JUNE 24.

D. Walked to Itchen wood by the larch wood, which had sad notes of nightingales afraid for their young in it. The ground is all over broad, smooth wood grass and creeping traveller, and white violet leaves are hidden. It is poppy time, they mix nicely with white campion, and look out from the tops of hedges pretending to be tree poppies. Mallows and cranesbill look nice together.

Village children in the park at Avington

I looked at the Burrage place and picked some Burrage, and I got close to chucking parters in a thick hedge. I think there were littles. There has been a great deal of west wind for a week. For three days it has been too cold to sit out.

JUNE 26.
E. Cold and dripping: thermometer can't get nearly to 60. The cuckoo's egg in the chalk pit has hatched, and we made it turn a little ball of wool out of the nest this evening: it did it with an appearance of strenuous persistent disgust. There are no roses yet: the Ayrshire has opened one bud, but all its others are far behind. The first month of the summer is nearly over and we have had hardly any heat.

JULY 6.
E. We continue to be here. D. has been away for only three days. At last the thermometer has reached 70. It rose to 71 to-day for the first time. We have a few pink roses, but no big blow. The first white and the first pink moss rose opened together to-day. Not one La France yet. The young cuckoo is not yet fledged, but is large and violent. The swallows are only fledging to-day. The old bird began to sit on June 1, and the eggs hatched on the 17th.

Meadow Cranesbill

I went a long bicycle ride on Sunday with Ella Pease* by Kilmeston to Warnford, and thence by Wickham to Botley and back to Winchester by train. On the way down from London I saw two partridges rise from between the rails in front of a passing train: the cock was first just in time: the hen was a little later and was hit by the engine. I looked out of my train and saw the bird flapping just clear of the rails after the passing train had gone by. It happened just after we had passed Worting signal box on the way down. We are well into honeysuckle and sweet-briar time and the Lonicera is in flower.

JULY 10 (SUNDAY).

E. Our last day: we seem to be going almost before the summer has begun, and yet it is only one week earlier than last year. Honeysuckle is past its best, Lonicera just come to it and plenty of sweet-briar flowers are left, but very few flowers of the Ayrshire rose are out and not a single lime flower yet. Turner's crimson rambler is in flower: there has been no big blow of roses except on the Rêve d'Or: many of our plants haven't yet opened a bud. Indeed we shall have gone not seeing what many of our new teas are like and having only had the first blooms of the earliest. I have only been here on one day this year when the thermometer has touched 70. To-day has been gloomy and cold, not nearly up to 60, but the sky cleared in the evening, the sun set visibly and there was a lovely soft mist in the water meadows. We took a most tender leave-taking walk round the larch copse, where we saw a brood of long-tailed tits all round the place where the first nest was found building this spring, and found five young tree pipits most compactly set in a nest in the larch copse chalk pit. There is a great field of poppies above the station—wonderful to see. Once again there has been a cottage blackcap singing all day, day after day, in our chalk pit. The young cuckoo is not fledged yet. The successful nests on our cottage this year have been (excluding sparrows, of which two pairs are rearing brood after brood), a swallow's, blue tit's and blackbird's.

English Partridge

* Daughter of Sir John Pease of Alnmouth; she was a great friend of the Greys and a Northumbrian neighbour. It took me some years to find an original copy of the *Cottage Book* and when it materialized the copy belonged to Ella Pease and was signed 'E.G.' March 1909.

1899

APRIL 27 TO JULY 9

THE HOSPITAL OF ST CROSS
FOUNDED AS A CHARITY FOR THE POOR IN 1132
BY THE BISHOP OF WINCHESTER

APRIL 27.

D. We came for the first time yesterday. Both thought we heard a faint sound of nightingale in the chalk pit, as we came through the gate, and later the bird was clearly heard to be there. It sang splendidly at night with a small moon. I got close and heard the full notes. It is there again to-day, but it is not thought to be safely established. We have been regularly taken in by long-tails. We heard them in the south-west lime tree and looked up for the nest. I said, seeing a square bump on a bough, "I suppose that's not it?" and E. said, "No, not that," and to-day after much watching I saw a tit go into the bump and stay there. It is high up but there is not much excuse. Two marsh tits* have been in and out of the smallest of the three holes where bats used to be.

Marsh Tits

APRIL 29.

E. It is a backward spring: chestnuts show a small tender green and willows, but one's eye searches in vain amongst the beeches for any sign of green—the beeches are all stern and brown: the elms are not green yet though it can be seen that life is stirring in their buds. As I walked into Winchester on the morning of the 27th the bees were humming heavily in the willows at the end of the path from Chilland. There is no drought this year and the fresh green upon the earth itself is thick. Blackthorn is in flower.

MAY 3.

D. I heard a great fuss of long-tailed tits, and went out and saw nothing: then the noise got worse and I looked up and saw a medium-sized bird with its head right inside the nest. I shood it away in a great hurry before looking at it through glasses, and then was puzzled what it was. It flew into a tree from which came the odd wryneck† noise that I have been trying to make out. Some time after I saw a hen chaffinch make for the nest twice, and the birds drove it

---

* Another example of the Greys' ornithological prowess – this time Dorothy's. The marsh tit and willow tit are extremely difficult to tell apart. Both are hole nesters; the marsh tit uses natural holes whereas the willow tit excavates its own.

† The bird's name comes from its habit of twisting its head right round on its neck. A member of the woodpecker family giving a shrill 'quee-quee-quee' call. It was a relatively common bird in southern England at the turn of the century but has declined steadily and mysteriously.

The River Itchen below St Cross Mill near Winchester

away with great fury. I thought the eggs were perhaps broken, but the birds came back very carefully, and the hen was fed on the nest.

MAY 10

E. The best day of the year yet and I am here for it. Shade temperature has gone up to 64: there is dry weather, but no drought, and the Itchen valley is full of luminous air and light green. It is a backward spring still and there have been many night frosts, night after night in May. Young beech leaves are to be seen at last but are still shy: the lime buds are showing green, but there are no lime leaves and the wild park is for the most part brown and bare: the great lime avenue looks as stiff as winter.

The nightingale is still in our chalk pit, but doesn't sing much—only speaks briefly. A week ago it sang from dusk to dawn. We have refrained from looking for its nest. Swifts arrived on May 6. The pair of swallows are visiting our porch again, and for a week have held much conversation in the porch, but there is no fresh mud put there yet. Bluebells have been brought to us. We heard a turtle-dove for the first time this season to-day. Kingfishers are clamouring up and down the Hiddin.

Chaffinch

MAY 15.

E. Chestnuts and beeches are beautiful: the spikes of chestnut flower are beginning to show amongst the thick green of the leaves and the Micheldever beech avenue has burst into brightness: it was all brown last week. Yesterday I bicycled past Middleton, through Longparish, up the Test to Whitchurch and lunched at the White Hart*, where I had not been for thirteen years; I sat in the well-remembered little room and recalled many things: it was there that I read for my final schools alone, and fished the Test: it was there that I fished before we were engaged, and it was there that we used to stay in our first year together. As I was coming over the hill from Itchen wood rain came on, but the tame park looked bright and glad of the rain, the leaves have light in them now even when the sun is hidden. Lilac is out.

Thuja

MAY 27.

E. Two days ago winter threw a look backwards from the north and the north wind is blowing cold still and conquers the sun. Forty-nine and 33 have been the maximum and minimum of the last twenty-four hours. But we are in the middle of the chestnut flower, which is very fine this year, the great chestnuts at the entrance of the tame park are glorious and the flowers on the top rise up against the sky and are moved by the breeze. Hawthorn is also out at last. One night in this week we were disturbed by scrambling of a heavy body in the trellis and walking in the roof and ill-omened squeaks and unfamiliar mutterings above our bedroom. In the morning I found a dead starling dragged under the trellis to the hole into the roof, where blue tits used to nest: its head and forepart were much eaten and when I pulled it away I thought small faces shrank back into the roof. We had the roof opened and found what we expected—a nest with two young stoats—a large nest made up with the materials of the blue tit nests and with remains of rabbits and numbers of birds. In this same night the chaffinches eggs were taken from their second nest: they have made one and abandoned it in the Thuja hedge and their second

* The White Hart is still in business in the middle of Whitchurch.

94

with four eggs was on the cottage: but I think the bird is all right and is now building on another side of the cottage on the foundation of an old blackbird's nest with the materials of the long-tailed tit's nest in the limes. We think the long-tails got off all right, but we know that the hen chaffinch longed for these materials before it was at all lawful to take them, and we think of fixing the tenth commandment in front of its nest as soon as it has begun to sit.

JUNE 12.

E. There has been great heat—seven or eight days of it in the early part of June. We have driven to Salisbury and Stonehenge and back: then to Amesbury and on to Littlecote, where we stayed a week and drove back yesterday by Whitchurch under a blazing sun. But to-day the heat is all gone, and there is a dull sky and cool wind. While we have been away summer has completely taken the place of spring. Chestnut flower has just fallen, wild roses are out and elderflower stares boldly at us. One or two honeysuckle flowers are out, but the aphis is overwhelming even the fine lock of it that hangs over our glass door, and which is generally free. The roses have improved greatly: we were in despair about them and are now more cheerful: they are poor plants, but our own and they are not dead and have some buds. The swallows have a nest and eggs under the eave behind the pump-room and the nest which D. saw the chaffinch building on the foundation of the blackbird's belongs to a spotted flycatcher. There is a fine nest of young blackbirds in the Thuja hedge*.

JUNE 22.

E. After at least three weeks of complete dryness rain came heavily two days ago—rain of all sorts—light useless rain, steady, soaking rain and prodigious showers. Everything is now happy. It is the time of wild roses and elderflower: yesterday we drove to where the road divides Itchen wood from Micheldever wood to

Stonehenge

---

* Otherwise known as western red cedar. The leaves give off a citrus odour when crushed or trimmed.

Sheep-dipping in the stream at Micheldever before the annual shearing

see the show of lady's slipper there, and we saw it and it was splendid, dazzling, and sweet. There was a little burrage too, which D. picked, and some in Itchen wood. But the burrage in the wood is far taller than that in the open waste land, and being taller and less concentrated its colour is less effective. Hardly any roses in the open yet— the first white moss is just out, the aphis on all the honeysuckle is now terrible, our big blow of it is quite spoilt. A thrush is sitting in the chalk pit and its mate sings all day (till 9.15 last night), but its song has lost the spirit of spring: it is very persistent but perfunctory—as if it didn't enjoy its own song much, but had to sing because the other would go on sitting. As usual a blackcap has now come to our limes and sings there most of the day as he flits and feeds: but his song ripples with gladness, and sounds as if he were careless, and glad, and free, and had got rid of all duty. Blackcaps have a spell of continuous singing for some days just about this time every year. About a week ago I found an empty reed warbler's nest above the wagon bridge: to-day it has three reed warbler's eggs and a cuckoo's of the usual colour.

Blackcap

96

JUNE 25 (SUNDAY).

E. I protest that D. might write more than she does in this book: I am sure Elizabeth* would.

Could anyone do a more summery thing than to lie in the middle of a mass of yellow lady's slipper and listen to the bees in it? At any rate, that is what I did this afternoon. It wasn't quite perfect because the sun was not out, and the scent of lady's slipper needs the sun to bring it out. For a moment I felt like a senseless field beast for lying down in such flowers and crushing them, but my doing so was a very proper tribute to the profusion of nature. In a garden where flowers are grown by the square foot it would have been a crime, but to the north of Itchen wood nature gives ladies' slipper by the acre. So I lay in it and put my eyes level with the flowers and listened to the bees.

JUNE 27.

D. After having been for that long driving about, the cottage seems even smaller and snugger than before. You think of the wide country, and place your cottage better. We have taken to sleeping out at last, having always meant to and never bringing it off. I wake up a nice lot and enjoy my night. When a trout jumps and splashes flat it sets all the sedge birds[†] noising. A heron has croaked both nights, and coots sounds are very various. I got the little breeze that says "the dawn—the dawn," and died away. The larks are first, you wouldn't think they could see their way up in the dark: then every sedge and reed warbler makes monotonous, ugly noises, then swallow, and last thrush and then you go and sit on the bridge and notice the light. Swallows skim long before you see a swift, but these did not come out of the clouds for me. At this time of year small things drop out of the tops of the limes all night and fall through the leaves. I thought, too, I heard light bat wings in and out. Last night was E.'s first night out, and about 1 a shuffling was heard to hurry in and the mattress had to be carried in from rain, so the night was not very successful.

Note. Elizabeth did not sleep out.

Coot

* Probably a reference to *Elizabeth and Her German Garden*, by Elizabeth Mary, Countess Russell.
† The sedge and reed warblers. In the chapter titled 'The Return of the Warblers' in *The Charm of Birds*, Grey relates how he liked to start the reed warblers singing by throwing a pebble into the river; 'a moderate disturbance will start reed warblers and also sedge warblers singing'.

JUNE 28.

D. A thunderstorm at 6 o'clock, great rain, and very peculiar hailstones, quite round, pure hard ice, radiating from the middle. About two of these would go to a thrush's egg in size. I picked up a handful and rattled them; it felt funny, and they were delicious to eat. I should think that there were about forty on the grass in front. They broke as they fell on the roof.

Note. Elizabeth does not dare to hoe, for fear of being thought odd: whereas I mowed my cottage lawn and weeded my cottage roses all myself for many years.

JULY 9 (SUNDAY).

E. To-morrow we go and to-day we have been taking sad leave of the cottage, and meadows, and valley. We went to the ash and sat there in the evening. The cottage has been a dear friend to us this year: we are very grateful, and perhaps all that happened before we came this year has made us more than usually fearful and sad at leaving it. We are going rather too soon—in the full magnificence of midsummer. Nothing is stale yet: the full blow of roses is at its best: the lime flower is opening fast and the bees hum in it, and there are whiffs of its scent in the air. Wild roses are still common though failing, and the thrush still sings: at sunrise to-day there was some quite loud singing. Our last days have been fine summer days, warm and light. On Friday there was a very heavy rain and some thunder: after it was over I went up to the Aquarium and found the cuckoo's egg hatched, and a fat, black, hideous young cuckoo wedged in the bottom of the reed warbler's nest. Everything was still and dripping: there were steady pink clouds in the sky, very far away, and against them I saw two herons crossing the valley with their slow, springy flight, so far away and high up that they seemed to belong to another world and to be unconscious of this one.

Herons

1900

March 17 to July 3

St Catherine's Hill

Overlooking St Cross and Winchester, classic chalk downland once
famous for its black-faced sheep and wailing plovers

MARCH 17 TO 19 (SATURDAY TO MONDAY).

E. We opened cottage for the year and came at midday and went for a walk up the wren path to the Aquarium. It was very cold, but with some sun, and when the sun came out we sat down in it and were warm. Birds not singing much, but wrens sang and proclaimed their path. We heard the first pair of long-tails in the wren path and saw them fly to the island opposite and build at their nest in the fork of an oak, high up. They are protected both by height and water from all humans. Other sets of long-tails were about in other places, but were not building that afternoon.

The reeds near the Duke's corner are beautiful; no leaves, but a forest of bare yellow canes with fine plumes, which are silver grey in sunshine: we sat down amongst them and looked through them; some are taller than others, but all have beautiful plumes and seem pleased, hardly proud, but very conscious of being graceful. It can only be by some special care of nature that such graceful things have survived the snow and storms of last winter. January and February have been very wet and the river is strong and full. Some sweet-smelling coloured violets are out in the wren path and the white ones in the oak meadow, but elsewhere only leaves. On Saturday night the thermometer fell to 19; Sunday began bright and still, but east wind came and covered the sun with clouds and in the afternoon there was heavy snow. D. was caught by it in the larch plantation; I reached the black farm in it on my way home and lay there under a straw stack in perfect shelter from wind and snow for a long time, but the snow seemed endless and at last I got up and ran home.

We have not found many changes, but some trees have been cut down by the wagon bridge, and an offensive railing*, for which no use is apparent, has been put across the wren path under the big chestnut. The people who live here don't love this place as we do, or they would not do these things.

APRIL 28 TO 30.

D. Came here alone on a perfect day, not a breath of wind, no cloud, birds in full spring song. The limes are in the largest kind

Yellow Violets

---

* This is how I finally proved the identity of 'wren path'. A century later a rusty old iron fence still remains under a huge chestnut tree.

The estate sawmills in Avington Park

of bud, but not yet spickley. Drinking poplar small white leaf but hasn't any shade under it, cherries in wild park dropping petals. The old early willows by hiddin brook are asserting themselves after their cutting. A thrush has a neat nest in a bunch of mistletoe on one of the near limes. I found a tittick* nest high up in the largest oak behind the cottage. A chaffinch is sitting in ivy on a front poplar, a wood-pigeon is sitting in the larch wood, and a silly robin is in an old tin pot stuck up in a lime tree in avenue. I heard about all the summer birds that belong to the time and the place in the first half hour of being here. Wood wren in wild park by large ash pit and kinglets in their proper place. There was an unusual lot of yaffling† in wild park and lots of lesser spotteds. There is a nightingale in the chalk pit, in the wheelwright's garden, and in the oak meadow, one can't be sure of their staying at this time of year, it may even be that they are really all one bird.

* Long-tailed tit.
† The laughing call of the green woodpecker.

Cherry Blossom

MAY 5 TO 7 (SATURDAY TO MONDAY).

E. This has been BEECH Sunday*; wherever there are beeches their tender green meets the eye and satisfies it. We have also had two warm days, one fine and one softly wet. Birds have sung gloriously, the air has been so full of sound that it has been difficult to listen to any bird separately. Two nightingales, one in the chalk pit and the other in the oak meadow, filled the cottage with song last night; it seems to be a great nightingale year. A wryneck, which kept coming to the broken poplar in front and making a noise, has been caught with the binox looking out of a hole near the top and being shy. Of two greenfinches, which were both building, the male was collecting moss and the female wool only, on the ground close together. I visited the kingfisher place; one of the holes is dirtier than ever and a kingfisher, looking more brilliant than ever, flew out of it and away up "Hiddin," and when I looked into the hole I could see eggs. I saw spotted flycatchers to-day, one arrived at the cottage and I think turtle-doves and shrikes are all that have to come now.

Primroses

Limes and elms are not green yet; geans, primroses, and blackthorns, are still in fine flower. Bluebells are beginning, but beeches are best of all: the tame park with sun on it and soft rain about it looked wonderful from the hill opposite.

We have sat out for late tea both nights.

MAY 10 TO 14 (THURSDAY TO MONDAY).

E. A warm day, a cool day, and a very cold Sunday, never above 46, which nearly silenced the birds with a dry hard north wind. There is no shade yet under the limes and oaks and ashes are not green. A pair of missel thrushes have reared a brood in our limes; the young look very large and uncomfortable and stand upon the nest. A lark has hatched in a cart rut in the open grass field above the cottage; it has sat amongst the feet of all the cows, which are in the

---

* The second Sunday in May. See page 127 of Grey's autobiography *Twenty-Five Years* for a charming description: 'There are a few days in the first part of May when the beech-trees in young leaf give an aspect of light and tender beauty to English country which is well known but indescribable.'

field every night. There is a great sight of cowslips in the tame park; we picked a lot one evening. Turtle-doves* have come this week.

MAY 19 TO MAY 23 (SATURDAY TO WEDNESDAY).
E. Sunday was fine and I went a long bicycle ride. Coming from Whitchurch I spied the open country for stone curlews† and at last saw one standing in young corn; after some manoeuvring I got to within about 150 yards and saw two; when I tried to get nearer they ran and crouched and disappeared. A year ago we saw one stone curlew fly low over the road in this park as we were driving from Whitchurch; now the season has come round again and I have been to the same place on the chance of finding stone curlews. I count this a great success.

Last week was very cold; now we have had stormy south wind and one wet day. The hawthorn is not out yet, and the chestnut flower is only beginning and the leaves of the limes are still too small for shade. Bluebells and bog beans are fully out.

MAY 25 TO 28 (FRIDAY TO MONDAY).
E. Warm days and fine; the earth has been well soaked too, and everything is set towards summer. This has been Lilac Sunday, and hawthorn, chestnut, laburnum, whin, and broom, are all in flower.

We have had another success with stone curlews. We drove over together on the chance of seeing them. I could make out nothing in the special place in the young corn, but far away on the fallow I made out a bird of the right colour; while I was trying to get it against the sky line, it rose and flew and lit just where I first saw it a week ago. D. then went to the copse in the field, while I stayed with the horse, and had a good look at it. We dined at Whitchurch, and had a walk first down the river where we used to fish so long ago.

JUNE 4.
D. To-day has been warm after four very cold days. A goldfinch is finishing a nest in a lime branch just in front of kitchen window. I have been up in the high fields to the north

Cowslips

---

* Europe's only migratory dove, returning from its African winter quarters in early May.
† Now very rare in Hampshire; much of their favoured chalk downland has been ploughed up. Today they are concentrated on the dry sandy heaths of Breckland and east Suffolk.

The lodge keeper's wife and daughter beside one of the park lodges at Avington

every evening at dusk to listen for stone curlews. Once I thought I heard a cry that I did not know. Two notes, the second four notes higher than the first, ending long and clear, much higher than a plover which I heard at the same time. Lying very still under a hedge, two hares came to within a yard of me, suddenly got frightened and rushed away, their feet making quite a thundering on the dry field.

Hedge nightingale still in full song.

JUNE 11.

D. The nightingale left off its night singing, but still sings a little in the day.

Brown Hare

JUNE 25 (MONDAY).

E. The season has become very late; our honeysuckle is not nearly out; one or two advanced bits are in flower, but that is all. The Ayrshire rose is just as backward and about a dozen roses only have opened in the beds. I picked the first white moss to-day. Plenty of thrushes sing still, blackbirds can be heard, a cuckoo to-day had its note still clear, loud and perfect. The nightingale in the oak meadow sang

loudly and much on the night of the
15th and was heard to utter broken
little bits of song on the 21st,
22nd, and 23rd. Lots of other
birds sing, but we have had no
cottage wren or blackcap this
June and I have heard fewer
wrens than usual this season.
Tree pipits do not come to these
meadows, as they used to do. The

Turtle-doves

goldfinch in our lime sits very well and to-day in landing a trout* I disturbed
a turtle-dove in a bush. It had a nest of eggs and D. and I went in the evening
and saw it on the nest without disturbing it. But we have had much less
crooning of turtle-doves, than we think is due to us, this year.

There has been constant wind and rain and coolness, we have not been
able to sit out in comfort any day that I have been here; but we are glad to have
no drought and do not complain. Only on each successive pouring day I wish
there had been a drought, that the splendid rain might be less wasted and
more appreciated.

Yesterday I bicycled to Blackmoor under a moist unsettled sky, but not in
actual rain. I had to come back on very wet roads against wind and thick fine
rain. It was unpleasant while I was dry, but when the wet had thoroughly
soaked in, so that my skin was all equally in touch with it, and when I came to
a magnificent wood where the trees were all receiving the soft June rain
gratefully, and passing it on quietly and kindly to the bracken below which
was such a bright happy green, I began to understand and feel things. And
then I became part of it all and found my place in it and loved the softness of
the rain; and it was delightful to be warm and wet and I would not have
changed the day for any other.

JUNE 27.
E. As I was shaving this morning I saw a cock cirl bunting sitting on the
acacia in front of the window; it was looking at me with the uneasy doubt of a
bird that has a nest and wants to go to it, but is afraid. Presently it went into
the Thuja hedge, stayed in it for a small time and came out and flew right

---

* One of the very few references to fishing, which is interesting as it was the major occupation
for Grey at the cottage.

away in a businesslike manner. Had it been any common bird I should have felt sure of finding a nest. I hurried my dressing, went out and found that the incredible had happened, and a cirl bunting's nest* was at our door. It has two young birds and an addled egg. We now have a goldfinch on one side of the cottage and a cirl bunting on the other.

JULY 3.

E. It rains every day, so much that we do mind a little, though we don't complain because it is so much better than drought. To-day I am going to London between the showers, but we had two minutes sun this morning and I stood in it and really felt it; it seemed quite strange. Sweet-briar is now well out. The cirl buntings are all right and I have had several watchings of them. The goldfinches are feeding their young too, but they feed at long intervals, they bring something which is invisible in their beaks and they take a long time to administer it to the young.

Cock Cirl Bunting

Our rose-buds are struggling into flower one by one, but they are very sodden and humble.

E. We left our dear cottage on Tuesday the 10th of July. D. and I had both been away in the week before, she only from Thursday till Saturday, and when she left the cirl buntings were all well. We both came back separately on Saturday afternoon and went together to the cirl bunting's nest. Both the young ones had been taken in that short interval of her absence. We had promised ourselves much watching of their feeding in our last days and perhaps the sight of their fledging and we were very unhappy. I think we minded a good deal more than the cock cirl, for I saw him next day; he perched in the poplars, and sang, and flew off gaily, like a bird glad to be free. A chaffinch's nest in the Travellers' joy was robbed of five eggs in the same time; we think it was jackdaws: I heard their ill-omened chatter close to us early on Sunday

---

* W.H. Hudson stayed at the cottage a few weeks later (see *Hampshire Days*, chapter 12) and wrote to Dorothy with the good news that the cirls were attempting a second brood. She wrote back in a state of great excitement, imploring him to protect the nest from the dreaded stoats.

The drive at Avington Park (the big lime avenue)

morning. We fear for the goldfinches; they too are gone from the nest, but they may have fledged. Young ones and old ones were about us all Sunday: they seemed an older brood, but they were many and the place was full of their flitting and tinkling.

In these last days summer remembered itself, and on our last evening we sat out late under the limes, with warm air about us and the moon above; it was the first such night this summer and it seemed as if summer were beginning, just as we were leaving. In May we had what we expect—spring weather, and we enjoyed it, but for summer we stake our cottage all upon June and there was no summer in June this year.

Sweet-briar is now fully out, the later and cleaner honeysuckle is only beginning: the Lonicera is fully out; the roses are hardly at their biggest blow; some of the highest lime flower is out, but very little. That was how things were, when we left our cottage, where we feel so hidden and safe and so sure of day after day. Now we are both in the open world and its unknown chances again.

Jackdaw

1901

April 27 to July 14

View from St Catherine's Hill
Looking south towards Southampton, where you see the
stream winding through the meadows below St Cross until it
is hidden by the tall rookery trees at Shawford

APRIL 27 TO 29.

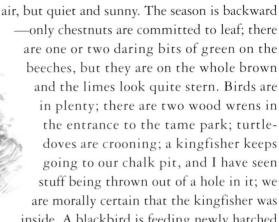

Blackbird's nest

E. A plain Saturday to Monday in a cold northerly air, but quiet and sunny. The season is backward —only chestnuts are committed to leaf; there are one or two daring bits of green on the beeches, but they are on the whole brown and the limes look quite stern. Birds are in plenty; there are two wood wrens in the entrance to the tame park; turtle-doves are crooning; a kingfisher keeps going to our chalk pit, and I have seen stuff being thrown out of a hole in it; we are morally certain that the kingfisher was inside. A blackbird is feeding newly hatched young at our porch, a chaffinch is building by our glass door; a wagtail* is laying and has now four eggs in an old blackbird's nest in the recess, and a thrush has deserted four eggs in the Thuja hedge.

MAY 3 TO 6 (FRIDAY TO MONDAY).
E. Warm days, fit for sitting out, but cold at night. We had late tea out on Saturday and had no stove till Sunday night. The blackbird deserted her young owing to a late mowing one night we fear, but to make up D. has found a robin feeding young in our grass bank. The wagtail is sitting and the chaffinch still builds. The kingfisher only seen once, but perhaps it is sitting or laying. Chestnuts are now thick and a beautiful green, and beeches are for the most part radiant; our limes are getting spotty.

MAY 10 TO 13 (FRIDAY TO MONDAY).
E. Warm and fine days, especially Sunday, and there has been rain in the week. The chaffinch sits on three eggs, the wagtail has just hatched, a blackbird (perhaps the same that deserted from our cottage) has built in one of our limes and is sitting: the kingfisher has been seen, but only once, to fly into the chalk pit with a fish in its beak, and there is a goldfinch's nest in the elder bushes in the chalk pit. The country is very beautiful especially with beeches, and there are still plenty of bare brown trees to give one happy thoughts of how much of the wonderful spring is still before us.

* The pied wagtail.

Net fishing at the trout fishery at Chilland

MAY 17 TO 20 (FRIDAY TO MONDAY).
E. Very warm fine days, but we want rain. I bicycled in some heat on Sunday to see Sir D. Barburn at Broxwood; it was a fine journey through differing country and by beautiful waysides. We found a linnet's nest in the field. This has been Lilac Sunday—our room has been full of it and very sweet. Chestnut flower is out, but the hawthorn not yet.

MAY 28.
D. We came here three days ago for Whitsuntide. It is very droughty and our lawn smells of hay. The hawthorn is poor this year, but foliage very good. The drinking poplar splendid. The three young chaffinches were taken away before breakfast on Sunday. On Monday a hen chaffinch was busy all morning pulling the nest to pieces, and moving it to an elder bush in the hedge running west, probably the

Goldfinch's nest

MILL BRIDGE. ITCHEN ABBAS. HANTS.

Cutting reeds with a scythe at Itchen Abbas Mill

same pair are building and they seem in a hurry. Another chaffinch in a lime close to kitchen door sat very badly at first, coming off sometimes every ten minutes, but it is more steady now. To-night there was only one nighter* to be heard in hedge half way along the road to the Norther's cottage. The cock that was in the oak meadow has not been heard at all this time. It looks as if the cocks wanted to try new nesting places and the hens don't turn up, and so the cocks have to go back to the usual larch plantation. There is a peewit† in the meadow opposite the cottage which is new and nice. It seems to fly in just the same way at night as in the day, and fussed very much as I sat on the bridge in dim moonlight. I suppose it finds its nest all

Peewit

* The nightingale, which has now become very rare in this part of Hampshire. The decline of coppicing is thought to be a major reason for their demise. The nightingale likes dense undergrowth close to the ground.
† Also known as the lapwing or green plover. Their numbers have recently declined to dangerously low levels as a result of modern farming techniques.

right in the dark. Have not heard a kinglet in chalk pit at all this time, but one is always to be heard in the usual place, and eggs can be seen in the nest. The honeysuckle is well out at Chilland. We walked to a large dingle towards horseshoe on Sunday. It is quite a wood, and full of birds, several nighters. I found a willow wren building and a bullfinch sitting. There is a linnet with young in a bush towards west gate, and a yellowhammer near it with eggs. Six rather poor Fortune's yellow roses are out high up on front of cottage. The room is still full of lilac.

JUNE 5.

E. I have been here for some days and D. has never been away. A new thing has happened—our Fortune's yellow rose has come into flower. There are over fifty blooms out at once on it, mostly quite high up and it is beautiful to see. We stand at a little distance in front of our cottage and admire; and we speak of it often every day.

Nothing bad has happened to the nests since the young chaffinches were taken, and that hen chaffinch is sitting down the hedge—again on three eggs only. A spotted flycatcher is sitting over my dressing-room window; it flies off when it hears the window open underneath it, and then comes hovering in the air to see what the noise was. In a walk up the wren path we found a blackcap, a dunnock, a bullfinch, a sedge, and a cock wren nest, very large and half lichen, half moss with one egg in it, which we took to be a cuckoo's. This egg has since been removed—has the cuckoo found out its mistake?

Hawthorn flower is just over; it has been particularly poor this season, but we found some particularly fine long arms thick with flower by the aish, and we brought them to our room, where they have been a great thing. Wild roses are just beginning and ragged robin and yellow iris are out, and the weather and everything is summer and very happy.

Ragged Robin

JUNE 12.

D. Came back from Littlecote, land very dry and a hard, cold wind. A great deal of young bird feeding going on. There seems to be difficulty in getting it done owing to the ground being so hard. Blackbirds and thrushes seem hard hearted. I saw a hen blackbird eat several things herself in the face of a screeching young bird who hopped feebly with wide beak. The noise made by two young blackbirds was painful all afternoon. Robins don't seem to suffer as much, and the young only make a noise in the crisis of the feed. A willow wren feeds very attentively, looks anxious with full beak when the young bird in the grass is found to have moved. I expect blackcaps are very kind.

JUNE 16 (SUNDAY).

E. It is full summer "and the green is deep." The grass is flowering in the water meadows and changes much of their green to seed colour, in which there is the gleam of buttercups and yellow iris to be seen, and the purple thistles are beginning to look proud. I went a long walk with Charlie to-day, to the horseshoe valley and back by Ovington; on the downs one cannot miss the strong pink colour of patches of thyme and with it the yellow of ladies' slipper, and other bright yellow down flowers. The elder and wild rose are out, our honeysuckle is just opening and our roses beginning; there are one or two breakfast roses every morning. The Fortune's yellow is still covered with flower—more than ever. We have been embarrassed by cirl buntings; the cock is constantly singing in our poplars*, but makes long flights away in all directions; he has a hen with him, but they both seem wild and restless and nestless. We have had very nice individual bird songs about the cottage to-day. A blackcap and a wren sang constantly about us all the morning, and a treecreeper threw in its wisp of song now and then. We have always had either a cottage blackcap or wren at this time, but now we have both. The general singing is dying down; the thrushes are weak, and the blackbirds, who seem to penetrate and string up the whole morning chorus of song, are silent.

Purple Thistle

* They are still to be seen down by 'Grey's bridge'.

JULY 2.

D. There has been much rain during the last three days, and on Saturday night we watched very splendid lightning after it got dark. It stretched right across in front of the cottage, from east to west, and the thunder was far off for a long time. Some rain fell that night and a good lot on Sunday. I walked towards Itchen wood and saw dew ponds filling and roads full of running water. Monday was wet and warm, and to-day there has been more thunder and heavy rain. It has been a splendid break up of the drought, our lawn seemed to get green at once, and the buds of the lime flowers looked grateful. I walked over Itchen Stoke down to Abbotstone. The old farmhouse looked very nice, and the small stream was very busy. There was some musk by the bridge. The down flowers are at their best. Linnets were singing slowly in the brushwood clumps.

Grasshopper Warbler

JULY 7 (SUNDAY).

E. My time has been sadly broken by politics. Our little plot of ground has been very rich in bloom; there are plenty of roses, honeysuckle, and Lonicera, and have been for a fortnight. The Ayrshire is now in very fine flower; sweet-briar bloom is going over; lime flower is just beginning and privet and brambles are in flower in the hedges. We have taken to feeding the birds with bread, and several sorts come, and don't seem to mind our not having done it before all these years. Even the wagtail eats a crumb or two.

JULY 14 (SUNDAY).

E. This is our last day here together, for D. goes to Fallodon to-morrow. It has been a fine summer day, and we went a nice meadow wander down Chilland to Easton Bridge, and picked wands and went to the Aish*. Everything is very dear and beautiful and restful. The lime flower is out, and the bees are amongst it, and the roses are still very gay, and the Ayrshire is

---

* Maybe the large ash tree in the chalk pit.

A shopkeeper's delivery cart pauses on the bridge over the River Itchen at Easton

still good and Turner's crimson rambler, and Jacmanni and Ophirie are in flower. The wagtail has laid four eggs and is sitting in the blackbird's nest by the porch: it has now sat on three sides of the cottage this year, in the blackbird's nest in the recess, and in the Travellers' joy, besides where it is now. Goldfinches, greenfinches, sedgebirds, reed buntings and a cirl are the birds that still are much heard, and it has been a great turtle-dove time.

E. I went to Cottage on Wed., Aug. 14, for one night alone to take leave. D. was at Fallodon, and I wrote about it to her*. I had a very touching time. It was a very wet evening and night. I felt so much that I seemed to live many days in the time.

Greenfinch

* 'It's one o'clock and I have just got here and I feel as if my heart was too full and might burst; the place is so sacred. I move about it in the most touching way. I feel as if I must keep coming in every half an hour to write to you. I have been on the bridge and eaten my figs on it and thrown the stalks into the river. I can hardly breath for the sacredness of the place. It is very strange that you aren't here; stranger than I thought, but I suppose it wouldn't be so strange to you, as I am so often away. What wonderful days you must have here without me!'

1902

March 8 to November 27

Near Shawford
Below St Cross the Itchen divides its stream. The main
branch flows on past Twyford, while the lesser heads to Shawford
about three miles from Winchester

MARCH 8 TO 10 (SATURDAY TO MONDAY).

E. A wonderful and happy Sunday for the time of year. Temp. 54 and 44, just the average of the beginning of May; gentle west wind and gleams of warm sun. The birds shewed and sang, and were building; a pair of long-tailed tits are building close to us in one of our limes, and another pair in wren path: a missel thrush's nest and a common thrush's are being built in wren path—the missler's a very loose affair of moss. The singing was good in the early morning; the blackbirds gave fine tone and quality to the chorus then, though we heard little of them in the day; misslers* sang a great deal in the day and tree creepers, chaffinches, thrushes, and dunnocks; tits made all sorts of noises; a goldfinch chirped in our limes as if it recognized us and the place, and a stock-dove flew out of an ivied tree—all well-known Itchen things.

D. found one or two violets; we walked to Ovington by black farm and river path, and pruned our creepers, and meadow wandered in the evening with the sun setting right down the valley, and everything very soft, and gentle, and happy.

Our drinking poplar is in great flower—covered with soft, reddish tassels, so many that it drops some upon the ground.

MARCH 15 TO 17 (SATURDAY TO MONDAY).

E. An even better Sunday; temp. 55 and 38, but still. We pruned a lot and lay out in the wild park in the afternoon near a flock of "chucking" fieldfares[†], which are not familiar Itchen things, not belonging to the season. The birds sang more confidently than ever, and in the morning, standing on our lawn, I was ware of a well-known sound, small and weak, but very sure, and there was a chiffchaff[††] in the chalkpit. The 16th is an early date for this.

There was some wind in the week, and it has blown out the tittick nest in our limes, but there is still plenty of time in the season for things to begin again.

Mistle Thrush

* Mistle thrush.
† Winter with us in Britain; these birds were probably moving north to Scandinavia where they nest.
†† Our earliest spring visitor along with the wheatear and sand martin.

April 19.

D. Got here at 1. Warm, windy, gray day. I planted some red and yellow willows in the hedge to the left in front and near the kinglet place. I heard the first willuck* sing just as I opened the gate on arriving, and saw swallows and heard a cuckoo and blackcap all at once. There are five wagtail eggs in the old blackbird nest in the alcove, the inside has been made up very loosely. There is a blackbird sitting calmly on a nest put right in the "shooting" in the corner by our bedroom window, we shall have a bad time when rain comes and so will it. There is a thrush nest with one egg in the east honeysuckle.

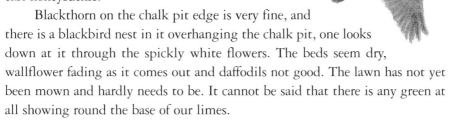

Fieldfares

Blackthorn on the chalk pit edge is very fine, and there is a blackbird nest in it overhanging the chalk pit, one looks down at it through the spickly white flowers. The beds seem dry, wallflower fading as it comes out and daffodils not good. The lawn has not yet been mown and hardly needs to be. It cannot be said that there is any green at all showing round the base of our limes.

April 19 to 21 (Saturday to Monday).

E. We think badly of the wagtail's nest—there are five eggs still cold. All sorts of birds sing, willow wrens, blackcaps, nightingales, whitethroats, cuckoos, and once one bit of grasshopper warbler. Both our days have been soft, and warm for the time of year; temp. going from 55 to 45.

April 26 to 28 (Saturday to Monday).

E. A strong N.E. wind has rather disturbed us, and discouraged the birds, which have sung very little; it has blown some mistletoe off the limes on to our lawn and to-night when I looked out and saw cold stars and brown trees and stood in the wind I felt wintry. But we had a wonderful afternoon; the sun came out and we went up the wild park to the bluebell place and down deep lane and stood and walked in the sun and out of the wind amongst primroses, wild violets and anemones in great profusion; the wood was bright with these colours, the ground being rather bare still and the flowers, even the violets, being not the least hidden. A few bluebells were out and we picked one and

* Willow warbler.

smelt it and put it away because the smell carried us too far into summer and we don't want to hurry the year. A dunnock sits on five eggs in the sweet-briar; the wagtail has deserted its eggs and one of them is broken. Chestnuts and sycamores alone amongst trees have small leaves; one or two precocious beeches show some green, but woods of beech are quite brown: elms are spickly, limes are brown, but their buds are large. The blackthorn is very good; it is very conspicuous, but with a slender grace, as if meant to show how bright it could be without being thick or luxuriant like hawthorn.

Whinchat   MAY 3 TO 5 (SATURDAY TO MONDAY).

E. We got into sun in the afternoon on Sunday, but otherwise it was cold, 32 and 34 at night and I think not 50 in the shade. I feel as if the best of the weather was keeping for us. Leaves push on, but half the beeches are brown and the limes not more than spickly. We walked to the downs beyond Linnet Farm and pryed about in their thickets and D. saw whinchats* for the first time, but we didn't hear them sing. These thickets are better than I knew and full of nice birds, having many sorts of birds in them from pheasants to lesser whitethroats. The cottage blackbird has fledged its young, the thrush in the Thuja has hatched, the dunnock has deserted and a greenfinch is building at our porch.

MAY 10.

D. Went to linnet down, stayed there from 11 to 4. Could not make sure the whinchats were building. There is a small beginning of a nest which might be theirs. Found five linnet nests with eggs and a wheatear's† nest with eggs. I watched the hen bird several times and lost her; at last, after the cock had been alone for about half an hour she appeared and played about, running out from a small depression in the ground and flying back to the same centre, and doing

---

* A summer visitor that is now rare in this part of Hampshire. Modern farming improvements are behind their decline; they favour moist uncultivated habitats.

† A summer migrant also rare in this part of Hampshire now that the downs have been ploughed up; they favour breeding territories in our upland regions above 1000 feet. In Victorian times thousands of wheatears were trapped as they rested on the south coast during migration, as they were considered a dinner-table delicacy.

Long before the days of herbicides, Mr Lampard, a shopkeeper from Cheriton
(in the panama hat), his wife and his brother take a Sunday afternoon stroll through
a meadow of wild flowers

the same in different directions, always flying back to the same place; the runs were about four feet long I should say. The cock took no notice. Then she flew a long way to a patch of green grass, made two flights straight up in the air a yard or two and down to the same place, and dived into a hole. I went and found the nest about two feet from mouth of rabbit hole which *Wheatear's eggs* runs along the ground, not deep, no bird was on the nest, and I got out a lovely egg to look at and put it back, and the bird made no movement. Then I felt a little to the side of the nest and she fluttered softly against my hand, about a minute after I took my hand away she came out and flew off. I saw one stone curlew and picked up one of its feathers. I noticed that a lesser whitethroat has some sharp squeak notes almost like a mouse in grass. It makes one or two of them separate from its ordinary

Sheep on local chalk downland

whitethroat singing and from its jabbering. These notes are quite unlike any other bird noises I know about.

MAY 10 TO 12 (SATURDAY TO MONDAY).

E. D. came on Friday and her exploits on Saturday overshadowed everything else. The weather is still cold, but the strong wind has ceased and there is no drought. Some young beeches in most tender green, others not out enough yet. Our lime avenue spotty, the big one bare and brown.

MAY 16.

D. Astridge told Susan that there were 9° of frost on Wednesday night. Some young beech leaves look rather shrivelled. It has rained nearly all day to-day. I found a goldic* nest in an elder bush in the west hedge, after long watching. Had a great hunt for the fair lark's nest last night but couldn't find it. To-day there is no fair lark to be seen, and I am dread-

Skylark

* Goldfinch.

fully afraid I may have trampled on the nest. There is a thrush nest new in the Ayrshire high up over my window, and a bunch of dead leaves tucked in a near lime seems to be turning into a cock wren nest. There is a slight beginning of a nest in the ivy. I have seen no flycatcher. I watched a fine wryneck in an old poplar, beautiful tight plumage, and inlaid lines on its back.

MAY 19.

D. I went to linnet down to find whinchats but there were none, and as I got up to come away I saw a stone curlew on the wing and another creeping into a whin bush. I watched it for some time and saw it was not on a nest so I hid, and it at once went creeping low on the ground and sat down on a mole heap. I thought

Stone Curlew and eggs

this could not be the nest, and I watched it for an hour. Then walked to it, and though I thought I had my eye on it all the time I did not see it leave the place, but it was gone when I got there and I found two eggs on the side of a mole heap, lying with a few bits of chalk flint.

MAY 22 (A THURSDAY).

E. (The space above is left for D., who should have much to say.) We have been here since the 16th. The whole of May has been cold; the poor sun has had no chance; the north wind has blown strong and ruled every day and there have been heavy bitter showers; I think these meant to be unkind and little knew how we rejoiced in them for being anti-drought. Some of the young beech leaves have been curled and browned by frost; limes and elms have only small leaves; oaks have tiny leaflets only and oak woods look bare; our cautious old walnut hasn't put its leaves out and the acacias are waiting. Except the beeches, nothing seems hurt or offended, but they have an appearance of more reserve and less brightness than usual at this time. Flowers and blossoms don't seem to mind; chestnut has just come into flower and one can see that hawthorn buds will open soon; primroses, bluebells, violets and small things are very bright and fresh.

I hardly dare write anything about birds; I am so overshadowed by D. I went with her on Tuesday to be shown the stone curlew's eggs—we spied and stalked and crept and saw a stone curlew standing by a ragged lonely whin bush on the down, like a sentinel. As we got nearer, it trotted off with the step of a ghost in the evening light passed the nest and disappeared. In the nest we found one egg and one young bird hatched since the day before, which lay flat and uttered. Both the egg and the bird are coloured to match chalk flints that have been a long time amongst mole heaps. We daren't touch the bird or the egg and came away excited. After this how should the same book notice such things as that a pair of chaffinches come into our room for bread and that the hen feeds the young with it, or that there are robins' eggs in the alcove nest, of which the foundation and outside is blackbird—the middle wagtail—and the inside and top now robin-built; but these things are also true.

MAY 26 (MONDAY).

E. Since I last wrote we have had wonderful days—fine, warm and altogether perfect; the leaves are still young and bright especially the beech and we have been able to sit in warmth and see them and walk at ease amongst them. I bought a trailer* for D. and we have had successful expeditions in it.

JUNE 1 (SUNDAY).

E. A warm day ending with rain, which stopped in time for us to have tea out; while we were at tea the white owl[†] flew past hunting our side

Barn Owl

of cottage meadow and in a minute or two came back to the old walnut with an animal, which it eat on a branch; it took a long time to finish but we could not see its manners distinctly, because of the ivy, and we daren't move for fear of disturbing it. About nine o'clock in the evening we heard the Cathedral bells faintly in the distance, then presently a small cheer in Itchen Abbas, then the Itchen Abbas bells began and soon afterwards Avington bells; there were big guns in the direction of Portsmouth and it is clear that some excitement is about. We suppose it to be the news of peace[††].

* From 1898 to 1899 Dorothy was seriously ill with Graves' disease. For some years she was much of an invalid and this would explain why Grey went on bicycle rides on his own. He also used to take her about in a trailer attached to his bike.
[†] The barn owl.
[††] The end of the Boer War.

Cattle and a goat being driven to pasture across the bridge at Itchen Abbas

Things have grown very much in the last week; hawthorn is fully out; the lime leaves make shade and are a very beautiful light green, ashes, the walnut and acacias still bare; oaks thick leaves, but very small.

JUNE 6 TO 9 (FRIDAY TO MONDAY).
E. Rain and cold—45 at nine o'clock this morning. On Sunday we went to look for young stone curlews and found one old bird, which we think decoyed us away so that we never saw anything more. The nests here go on well—we have a greenfinch, thrush, blackbird, robin and willow wren all sitting or feeding young on our cottage: the willow wren is some height from the ground.

Stone Curlew

JUNE 12 TO 16
(THURSDAY TO MONDAY).
E. A very remarkable time— nearly two inches of rain fell, about one inch on Friday and on that day the

Hay-making beside the River Itchen at Martyr Worthy

Pink Chestnut flower

thermometer never got above 49; large young greenfinches were drowned in their nest in the Lonicera, the other nests are all right and the goldfinch in an elder in the field hedge has warm young. A pale sun has looked sadly through the clouds now and then; the earth is spongy and water comes up round one's foot at each step; our cottage is approached through slosh. The cold is even more remarkable than the rain. I went to linnet down on Sunday morning with Hudson*—one old stone curlew was found, which paid great attention to us and sneaked about; there are certainly young ones concealed there. Some chestnut flower still remains and the pink chestnut in the Avington road is very beautiful; there is still abundance of hawthorn flower. No sign of wild roses yet. Our Chinas are just out, and our Fortune's yellow, but it has hardly any bloom this year. Our cottage honeysuckle isn't near flowering.

* W.H. Hudson, the famous nature writer, who dedicated his book *Hampshire Days* to Sir Edward and Lady Grey. The inscription can be seen on the dedication page of the *Cottage Book*.

JUNE 19 TO 23 (THURSDAY TO MONDAY).

E. More than an inch of rain on Thursday night; the
first summer day of the month was on Saturday; the
thermometer got to 61 and it was fine and we had
tea out. Never have we seen so cold and wet a June
(we are glad there is no drought); our walnut and
other walnut trees are still only in small red
leaf—not green: the acacias are in very small
leaf—we are not near any honeysuckle flower or
roses, except Chinas; wild roses are beginning,
but the last of the hawthorn flower is still
white on some bushes. We passed lots of it on
Sunday when we had a most successful trail
above the horseshoe and into the valley of the
Meon and back by Cheriton.

JUNE 28.

D. There have been four hot days. Therm about 73
and a nice breeze all the time till sunset. A blackcap
has sung a little in the chalk pit but in bits as if it was   *Sedge Warbler*
still caring for young sometimes. The willow wren's nest on the cottage is very
tightly filled with young and no mowing is allowed near it. Two small bits of
lonicera are out, and just three perle d'ors and one la France. The pink chinas
are at their best and there are lots of small pale deformed W.A. Richardson on
the house. No Ayrshires or other roses. I was awake for the early singing to-day
and yesterday, and there was great difference between the two, hardly any
singing this morning. There was much sedge singing last night after the moon
got up about 12 o'clock.

JUNE 30.

E. I came from Novar* yesterday (Sunday). We are in full summer and it is very
nice to feel sun and heat and know that there is no drought. One bit of honeysuckle only is out yet and walnut and acacia leaves only half grown. Wild roses
are in full bloom. The willow wrens all fledged this morning. Blackcaps and
chiffchaffs singing a great deal, as they do after breeding business is over; many
broods of goldfinches about.

* The home of Grey's great friend Ronald Munro Ferguson on the Alness river.

JULY 4 TO 7 (FRIDAY TO MONDAY).

E. Weather quite perfect; we trailed to the lady's slipper place on Sunday evening and found it in full flower and lay in a deep soft patch of lady's slipper; its lazy scent rose round us as we walked. This piece of ground seems to grow nothing but flowers in its loose crumbly soil, there are viper's bugloss and wild strawberries, thyme; St. John's Wort and Ragwort still to come, but no grass; it is a very choice place. Broods of goldicks are all about cottage, tinkling continually; the cottage wren sings loudly and a blackcap often. One hears blackcaps in many places singing much now that they are free from the trouble of feeding young. Sweet-briar is out, and the lonicera, but our honeysuckle only at the very beginning, and roses not yet at their great blow.

JULY 17 TO 21 (THURSDAY TO MONDAY).

E. It has been cold, 53 and 42 on Sunday. The roses and honeysuckle are now at their full blow and the Ayrshire rose is very great. Our blackcap utters a few final notes occasionally and chiffchaffs go on in a quiet rather reminiscent way. I heard a hidden thrush sing two or three loud notes and stop suddenly as if it had forgotten for a moment that the time for singing was over. Starlings and other birds are in common non-breeding parties in fields from which the hay has been carried. A blackbird which came into the open for bread was in most deplorable moult. I found a lark's nest with two eggs.

We trailed on Sunday and saw quantities of Test musk about Cheriton. Lime flower is now out but it is poor, spoilt no doubt by the cold in May and June. How severely that was felt is shown by the lateness of things now; the struggle they had has delayed them all and spoilt some.

JULY 25 TO 28 (FRIDAY TO MONDAY).

E. A most violent wind on Saturday, which made everything very uncomfortable and has strewn the ground with a litter that looks like autumn; it has been cold again, not nearly 60 on Sunday; one can't help feeling as if summer was over.

Lady's Slipper

AUGUST 1.

D. A coldish day with thunder in the south. There
has been much squeaking of young wrens who
seem to work themselves round and round the
sweet-briar hedge and never to leave it. I have
twice seen a young chaffinch trying to sing, a
very poor attempt, throaty and with all the notes
on a level, but keeping the time of the ordinary
song. A young robin has been on the mat a great
deal eating bread, and a few other things come for
bread, but no blacker this time. There were sounds in
the roof as of a stoat last night.

AUGUST 5.

D. E. went away for good in the morning. I sat under limes
in a breeze and there was faint humming up above. A warm
evening, therm. 58 at 9 o'clock. I walked in wild park and
found it very thistly and black looking, found one good
stretch of ragwort. Pruned pink rose hedge and finished
the Ayrshire. The sadness of going away time settled on me
heavily. The time never seems right for going away.

Ragwort

AUGUST 9.

D. Going away with hope of being back here in October. It rained yesterday till
6 then came out fine and still. I walked up towards linnet farm and looked over
the parks. A low sun made the yellow corn and haystacks a brilliant red colour.
The cirl is still singing to-day, and I have heard last whispers of both chiffchaff
and willow wren. The sadness of leaving is mixed with uncertainty as to the
fishing lease and dread of having to go altogether. It would be nice to grow old
here and the partings would not be so poignant.

OCTOBER 20.

D. We came on Saturday, and it is not thought that we have ever been here at
this time of year before. Leaves on our limes are thin, but oaks and ashes are
quite green, and hedges are still thick. We walked up the hill towards Itchen
wood with the sun hot on our backs, and eat blackberries and nuts all the way
as we went. We lunched in a safe place on the south side of the wood on plas-
mon biscuits and grape fruit very good. The colours in the parks are not good,

Kings Worthy station on the Alton–Winchester branch line

(but) there is a very splendid water elder bush by jaw hatches that we saw to be very red as we wandered in a late light. To-day a new stove has been fixed in the sitting-room, and our poor old little til was stood out in the rain and looked very piteous. It has been very kind and warm to us though ugly and not very clever. The new one is nice to look at and shows much more fire, but I don't like it yet. It has been warm all the time, and the therm. is 58 to-day though the sun is not out. The meadows are uglier than has ever been seen before. The brown leaves dieing make them look black and rough and ungrassy. The lime leaves are beautiful on our lawn, all shades of cream colour and very soft. I have heard several bits of thrush song but no continuous singing. There have been many swallows seen; four young ones sit on telegraph wire near the bridge and look poor and unhappy. Nuthatches have been heard and dunnocks and grey wagtails* and of course robins and wrens. We picked a

Meadowsweet

* Grey wagtails would winter around the water-meadows.

bunch of meadowsweet by broad water and there is a good deal of scabious.

OCTOBER 21.

D. Such a lovely day I stayed till 12 train*, and wandered up big lime avenue. It has much more leaves than ours, and the west part is quite green as one looks up at it. Therm. got to 58 yesterday, and just got to freezing last night. It is 55 to-day with a nice breeze.

NOVEMBER 2.

E. D. has had to take refuge here and is to try to stay all November. We are asking a new thing of cottage, that it should be a home to us in late autumn. It seems bold and trying our dear cottage very high, but it has been so kind always that we trust it. We are let to begin well; the weather is warm and still 56 and 43 yesterday and this evening we meadow wandered and went to the Aish and sat there in twilight at 5 o'clock. The beeches opposite were bright in colour and seemed to have light in them, as if they had kept

Song Thrush

summer sun stored in the leaves. The November sun has just looked at us once or twice and smiled and gone in again. We drove to-day and let the horse loiter up the long line of beeches, which were brown and yellow; and we eat pears in the dogcart, it was very nice—but very different to our usual times.

The cirl sings and has been identified and watched: a thrush sang this morning in the chalk pit. A lot of flowers are in our room that have never been in cottage before; monbretia, dahlias and scentless autumn things, but there are some roses too.

NOVEMBER 6.

D. There was some rain yesterday, but every other day since I came has been fine and warm, mornings brilliant sunny till 12, then light clouds till evening. Therm. 55 and upwards, and nights warm and windy. I lie reading in the sitting-room with dead leaves rustling in at the window out of the dark. The

* From the little branch line station at Itchen Abbas.

meadows are being much dressed down, all orris and reeds cut and carted away to cover wurzels in heaps, the wagon comes loaded through the river by the bridge and reminds one of the hay carting in summer. Each meadow channel is cleared out with a spade, and the meadow looks green and more like itself without the tall rubbish.

NOVEMBER 27.

D. I go to Fallodon to-day, having been here nice and safe for four weeks. There have been two wet days only, and no other rain, no wind, a few nights frost quite slight, and many warm sunny days. Even now the therm. was 42 last night and about 50 all day. The near

Snipe

meadows are all mowed and have water in them and many snipe* come in them and make their noise at night. I put up one lot of at least forty, one evening. I have seen two water rails, and there is a sound to be heard which I think must be made by them: rather dabchicky with a slight tinge of rabbit squeal. I have tried to find out about it but it is difficult. The winter here is much softer than in the north, and it seems much easier for fine days to be warm, and for the sun to get through the clouds. Dear Hampshire!

* Sadly not a sight you would see today as the meadows are no longer flooded.

1903

MAY 2 TO NOVEMBER 28

THE CANAL NEAR BRAMBRIDGE

ONCE AN OLD THOROUGHFARE UP TO WINCHESTER. CENTURIES AGO THE
DISTANT BRAMBRIDGE WOODS SUPPOSEDLY POINTED TO ONE OF THE MOST
IMPORTANT BRIDGES OVER THE ITCHEN

MAY 2.

D. Came on a soft day and found cottage quite safe still. Heard a distant willuk for my first summer bird, then whitethroat and much chiffchaff. Limes have more bud than small leaves, but the sweet-briar is quite thick, and there is much green to be seen. A thrush nest under the alcove has two eggs thrown out and broken and one left in deserted. A robin has four eggs in a low-down remnant of an old blacker nest by porch, and is reported not to leave the nest when chimney is swept. I see another nest, and hear the usual wagtail excitement on the north side. It is wonderful to come here into full spring straight from Rosehall* where no spring was. It is like sinking down into a delicious pool.

MAY 2 TO 4 (SATURDAY TO MONDAY).

Chiffchaff   E. Neither windy nor cold but very wet. 1.60 inches of rain in twenty-four hours: everything is moist and happy, and birds are singing most joyfully. We have missed very little green. A great blizzard in April kept things back for us: no trees are green except chestnuts and willows, and they not thick. We couldn't see or watch much or find nests on Sunday or do more out of doors than get wet, it rained so hard. We have our same two pair of bread-eating chaffinches, and there are other birds, a blacker and wagtail and robins with the same lawn habits as last year, and everything promises well.

MAY 8 TO 12 (FRIDAY TO TUESDAY).

E. Cold and dull on the whole—very windy on Monday; N.E. wind, no sun and 47 max. The fishing was very good and the birds sang well except on the very cold day, but we didn't have much success with birds. The stone curlews are not on their down, nor are there whinchats there, our robin's nest is destroyed; we saw two titticks with beakfuls of food and a golden-crested wren[†] with a beakful of stuff, but they all baffled us and we couldn't find their nests.

---

* On the River Cassley in Sutherland. In *Fly Fishing* Grey writes, 'In 1903 the lowest part of the Cassley was let to me by the late Mr W.E. Gilmour, the owner of Rosehall. In that year, and the two that followed it, my wife and I spent each April on the Cassley, and became much attached to it. After her death and my entry into office I did not visit the Cassley for two years. My brother (Charlie) fished it in 1907, and in subsequent years, till 1926 inclusive, fished it with me whenever he was in England in the spring. He became very fond of the river.'
† Goldcrest.

We found two wren's nests with eggs in the wren path. Beech green is coming on quickly, but not at its best yet. I think the 17th will be beech Sunday.

MAY 15 TO 18 (FRIDAY TO MONDAY).

The 17th has been beech Sunday and we started fair with a new bicycle and restored trailer, but we barely got a trail, the weather was so bad. It blew from the S.W. and W. this time, but it was still cold, and there were driving showers of rain. The April blizzard too has left its mark; it has killed all our iris flowers in bud; some chestnuts are frost bitten; the lilac flower has failed so far, and the hawthorn looks very scanty: we found one or two sheltered bits of it out to-day and smelt them, very fragrant and fresh. A blackbird's nest in our Thuja hedge has been destroyed, but close to it a linnet is sitting on five eggs. Our cottage nests are very unfortunate, I think now it is rats that do the mischief, we hear and see them about our walls. I am planning measures, but haven't got further yet than missing one with a new little gun.

We trailed in the evening to the beeches and D. brought back some branches: in the afternoon we walked to the head of tame park, and wherever we went we looked at beeches, sat near beeches, and talked beech talk.

MAY 18.

D. Brilliant sun day, therm. 52. Sat out, but with a rug and coat. Stared at the young beech leaves in tame park and felt very green. A turtle* crooned on a long time, and the singing of birds was pleased to have the sun out.

MAY 22 TO 25 (FRIDAY TO MONDAY).

E. It has ceased to be cold, the sun has been brilliant and the therm. up to 65, but there has been a strong N.E. wind. We had a long trail on Sunday out on to the Meonstoke road and back by Bramdean and Cheriton, bringing back copper beech branches from the copper beech place†.

JUNE 5 TO 9 (FRIDAY TO TUESDAY).

D. FOR LONGER.

E. Strong and tiresome north winds and cool weather. We went a fine trail by

Goldcrest

* Turtle-dove.
† Between Bramdean and West Meon Hut on the A272.

Mr Westbrook, the wood dealer, and his family outside their cottage at Wield

Whitchurch, Longparish and the Bloodhound and Beeches on Sunday: beeches are quite dark and unlustrous now. Iris and ragged robin are flowering in the meadows, birds are flying about with beakfuls of food, blackbirds have quite stopped singing in the last few days; they stop very suddenly and almost all together; one pair came into our room with the chaffinches to eat bread. Wild roses and elder are out; hay is being cut. I lay in Chilland meadow yesterday waiting for the rise and watched the wind and buttercups: buttercups are a great success every year; each season seems to be a great buttercup season. I have caught two large rats, which lived on the cottage; we hope it was these that destroyed all our nests: the two blackbird nests, which are all that are left, are still safe.

Buttercup

JUNE 11 TO 15 (THURSDAY NIGHT TILL MONDAY).

[No entry for these dates.]

JUNE 19.

E. Weather! weather! weather! nothing but north and east wind and bitter cold and rain (which we don't mind). On the 14th the temperature was 45 at midday, and never got above 48 all day—we lit the stove, but had it covered up when we left, being sure such weather could not be equalled again in what was left of June. To-day we returned; it has rained all day, the wind has been worse and *the maximum temperature for the day* 45. It is beyond all bearing and belief our summer and cottage time is slipping away. We have no flowers now in our garden, except the first blows of suckil on cottage and a few scattered sweet-briar blooms. One blackbird nest has fledged safely—the cock fed the young with bread in the nest now in the bushes, the hen also sometimes. Our bread party is now very nice and varied and tame. We have four very tame spinks*, a pair of dunnocks, a pair of pied wagtails and their brood, which they feed with bread, and the blackbirds: these are our guests, and a lot of sparrows come and snatch, but never get tame: they have the manners of thieves.

Wild Rose

JUNE 19 TO 22 (FRIDAY TO MONDAY).

E. The 20th was fine, but bitterly cold and gloomy. Sunday the 21st was a splendid day—not hot, only 55 max., but sun all day, a light breeze and a fine summer sky. We trailed to Stockbridge and thence down the Test, stopping on its bridges and visiting its mills and noticing all the way that this was wild rose Sunday. We still hear blackbirds sing, though not near Cottage. We had a beautiful trail and came back by train from Romsey.

JUNE 28.

D. We have had three splendid days, therm. up to 75 and a breeze, and hot sun. The sitting out under the limes has been very perfect, and the stove is under the writing-table again. We sat on the jaw hatches last night and I found myself seeing a spray of Test musk near the two islands on south bank. Then two more bits were seen higher up sticking up proudly out of some floating weeds, so the musk has really arrived quite near Kettidge†. I found a large bed of it up by black farm, very rich and yellow and natural looking. It was thought nicer to sit under limes to-day than to go a long trail, and we think it was right.

E. We went a trail in the evening and found crowds of musk in the little stream below Swarraton; the stream was double lined with it: we walked down to it and sat gazing and talking musk.

* Chaffinches.
† The cottage.

JULY 3 TO 7 (FRIDAY TO TUESDAY).

E. Fine summer weather, but cool. We went to Fareham by train on Sunday and trailed back up the valley of the Meon. Honeysuckle, Lonicera, Rambler and Ayrshire rose are all out now and other roses. I forgot to say last week that we visited lady slipper place and found it had failed this year: the plant is there but flowering very poorly.

JULY 10 TO 13.

E. These were hot days, twice up to 76 and the lime flower began to come out and the bees to visit it. I heard a nightingale utter a distinct and clear bit of song in the chalk pit on the 12th and D. heard the same several times last week. Test musk is increasing about the river: we walked to Ovington by river paths on Sunday night and inspected all the bits of musk: the best beds of it are opposite each other near black farm. We have cottage blackcap and wren as usual.

JULY 16 TO 20 (THURSDAY TO MONDAY).

E. Fine summer days: we went to Wilsford* on Saturday and came back on Sunday evening. It has been lime flower Sunday and this evening being misty and still the air seems saturated with lime flower scent: we like it very much. Dunnocks are feeding young somewhere in the chalk pit with our bread: the pied wagtails are feeding young in a nest on our chimney also with our bread: this is their second brood. The cock blackbird has at last shaken off the last shameless full grown young which clung to him greedily, and life is easier for him.

We had very good views of the white owl in a meadow walk to-night: it all but pounced once within ten yards of us, where we should have seen what it did.

JULY 24.

D. Came for the last summer visit, much upheld by knowing that we shall be here again in November. There has been rain and the air is washed and bright. We meadow wandered with wands and felt very gentle.

Lime flower

* The new home of Edward and Pamela Tennant. Grey would marry Pamela nineteen years later in the little parish church. Edward Tennant was MP for nearby Salisbury from 1906 to 1910.

Children paddle in the river at Itchen Stoke

JULY 25.

D. The young wagtails make a loud noise when being fed, and the young flykes* can just be heard. Heavy rain in evening and night. Went a short trail round lady's slipper place and picked much scabious.

JULY 26.

D. Trailed by horse shoe valley to the unknown Owlesbury, and found it to have many beautiful trees, a windmill and a church. A warm day but some wind. The sight from the top of Morne hill was very clear and blue and distant. Found the Cheriton musk rather getting over. The wafts of lime flower smell were very rich as we sat under limes in the morning. Heard a black-cap whisper and much crooning.

JULY 27.

E. A soft wet windy day, very grey and melancholy. We walked about larches and familiar places, ending up with the Aish to take

* Spotted flycatchers.

Dunnock

leave in the evening. It feels as if we were taking leave of summer, and so we have of the best of it. There is still lime flower and the two nests—spotted flyke and wagtail—on our cottage. The trailer has been a great thing to us this year: we have seen many miles and wide stretches of country together, light green and dark green, and under the summer sun.

JULY 30.

D. Went away north. Had a very wet evening for the last. Valley all smudged and bridge soaking. To-day is bright. The ragged old blacker is spread in the sun to dry. Flyke nest all right, and wagtails certainly feeding, but not very busily, I should think at least one young got rain-killed. This dear cottage is very much a hostage to fortune. I wish I could feel that having had so much good in it I could bear not to have any more, but I have no feeling of that sort, and fret to think of the end, though with great thankfulness.

OCTOBER 24.

D. Came here alone on the 23rd. A fine evening with a new moon in it. Limes still thick with leaves, and a good many roses out, no autumn colours except in water elder. Sat out all morning. Therm. 52 gray sky and rain at night. We hear great things of the gale in September, but no trees are missing round about the cottage. We greatly feared for the Aish and the drinking poplar*, and it is good to find them safe. River very high, an inch or two above the bottom of our bridge, and making much noise against it. The garden is to be changed, and I feel nervous about it. Two martins and about six swallows were about Itchen Abbas bridge.

OCTOBER 31 (SATURDAY).

E. We are at last having a wet year and not only that, but a record wet year. The river is fine; not altered a bit in character, no noise except at hatches, no flooding or dirt or disorder, but with silent power in its stream. You can see that it enjoys itself and is perhaps a little self-conscious; it can hardly help expecting the meadows and bank-growing things to notice the full strong flow of its stream.

Spotted Flycatcher

* Probably just below the Cottage by 'Grey's bridge'.

It rains still, and this has been a very wet week, but the chalk sucks it all in and though we have mud, there is no standing water. Leaves are late on the trees and not colouring well; they are sodden and unripe. There have been real thunderstorms this week here and in many places; the season has become so unusual that it does

House Martins

one unconventional thing after another, but it is on the whole warm now and we don't think it unkind. Cirls, dunnocks, wrens and robins are all that sing yet and they not much nor loudly.

We are changing the garden—bringing new soil by railway from a distance, and digging and planning very boldly. We are also ruthless—I have pulled down all the traveller's joy—our first and largest creeper: I hope we shall not kill the spirit of the Cottage.

NOVEMBER 5.

D. A vast lot of titticks were round about me as I sat under limes. They stayed more than an hour, going round and round on the cottage, getting inside the trellis, dangling from the lonicera, and one knocked its head against the side window. Their tails looked rather cold, and they were shabby and small, but very happy. Very few leaves now on limes, frost at night, but the last four days entirely sunny and wonderful.

NOVEMBER 16.

E. It has been a fine month—never windy, hardly any rain and warm: we have had a fair share too of sunny days; there is a great deal that might be said in favour of November. There was a very sharp white frost, 6 degrees last night. One oak above cottage is still dull green: the elms by the broad water have been very fair and the small English maples in the hedges are bright yellow. Brown beech Sunday* was about a week ago. All limes are quite bare.

---

* In the chapter titled 'Winter Birds' in *The Charm of Birds* Grey writes, 'No tree in autumn is more noble and honourable than the beech. Its dark leaves at first turn yellow; but the last stage before they fall is rich dark brown. As in spring there should be a Sunday set apart for seeing the young green beech leaves in their first beauty, so there should be a "Beech Sunday" for the colours in the autumn. At Fallodon in an average year this is the last Sunday but one in October; in the south of England it is the first Sunday in November.'

The garden is being made; the chalk-flints are being persecuted out of it and Jeffrey loam and Surrey soil are being brought in. A very strong man is hacking holes in the chalk pit for lilacs.

NOVEMBER 27.

E. Cottage has been very kind and so has November. We came in heavy rain and I am leaving in rain, but all the main time of our stay has been good; frost days and sunny days and warm days—all dear with no violence of wind. We have worked tremendously at the garden; its shape now appears; the beds are all ready and the rose beds planted; the chalk pit has had lilacs and pink may trees and honeysuckle and even Felenberg roses forced upon it and much white chalk spread in its roadway shows how tremendous the struggle has been. I am a little afraid of having done so much: we have raised our hopes of the garden and chalk pit to a dizzy height and I feel we have given hostages to fortune.

The water rail* has shown itself to us at last, it made its noise and flew out from the reeds afterwards one day when we were on the bridge: it has been a great relief to us to know that this noise does belong to a water rail.

Yellow English Maple

NOVEMBER 28.

D. Going away on a fine grey day, very grateful for my cottage cure. The month has been full of beauty and meadow colours and soft days of wintry sun. Thrushes have sung well since the first week of November. The cirl has been about every day, and many kinds of wagtails go flitting by the river. There is a little hoarse-throated owl which we have loved very much. Once it flew over the valley hooting all the time as it went. I saw the rail again yesterday, and heard its sound many times, and the noise of dabchicks† is very dear all day and quite late at night. Five months is far too long a time to be away from cottage joys, and I am very homesick.

---

* Its call starts with a grunt and ends with a pig-like squeal.
† A spooky 'trilling' call.

1904

April 29 to November 29

Near Bishopstoke

An April shower bursting stormily over rustling poplars

APRIL 29.

D. I came yesterday straight from Rosehall, with a great sense of plunging into spring. We had heard one rather chilled willuc, and I had seen wheatears, but it was wonderful to find swallows taking themselves for granted, and to pick up the various notes all rich and plentiful. A nightingale in the chalk pit sings as if it meant to stay. I am hoping that it has noticed the new fence that keeps out the cows. If it nests we shall feel consecrated. The garden is promising and there is a very fine bed of poet's narcissus in chalk pit, but the meadows are best.

E. This was the best first of May that we ever had, warm and sunny, making everything very happy, us and birds and young new leaves. On Monday the second of May, when we had to go to London the weather turned chill and wet, as if to mark how favoured we were.

We have to garden many hours, the garden being now worthy of trouble. The enclosure of the chalk pit* is very successful; the narcissus has flowered very well in it already.

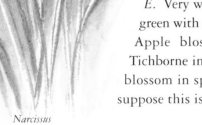

MAY 6 TO 8 (SATURDAY TO MONDAY).

E. Beech Sunday: we trailed by Stoke Charity and Sutton Scotney and back by all the beeches; the sun was shining and the beeches were very tender and high spirited. But there has been cold north wind and often a very gloomy sky and the birds have not sung as much as they did last time. We get on well with blackbird and thrush nests, but have found no others with eggs.

MAY 12 TO 16 (THURSDAY TO MONDAY).

E. Very warm days on 13th and 14th. Limes and elms green with small leaves, beech leaves thick and lustrous. Apple blossom wonderful, and one chestnut by Tichborne in blossom. It promises to be a great year for blossom in spite of last summer being cold and wet. I suppose this is so, because the blossom was very bad last

Narcissus

* In 1902 the Greys rented the chalk pit and fenced it to keep the cattle out.

year. The blackthorn has been good, but is now over.
These days have been apple blossom and tulip time:
the tulips in our new garden have opened to the sun.
We are still unsuccessful with nests. There is a linnet
in the Thuja hedge and one, which we think is a
linnet, though the eggs are different, in the field
hedge. The chalk pit is full of birds, blackcaps,
willow wrens, chiffchaffs, goldicks, dunnocks and
nightingales and wrens—at least one pair of each, and a
stock dove has a nest there. I heard a wood wren and
a kinglet in the wren path and saw a pair of tufted ducks
on the wild park water.

Tulips

MAY 14.

D. There have been two very warm feeling days, and the
green is at its best. We trailed to the copper-beech place
but they were not well out. The apple blossom is very fine
and makes one notice many little orchards not known of
before. I found a nice crab tree to pick from on the railway
embankment near the vicarage. A nightingale was singing to it, and it was
very pink and beautiful. The very old crab tree with small flowers in wild park
is quite wonderful. We saw it in a pink evening light, and loved it very much.

MAY 15 (SUNDAY).

E. One of the most magnificent May days ever known: sun and warmth and
light S.W. breeze. Chestnut has come into flower, iris has come out in the
chalk pit; the green has deepened and leaves grown thicker in a day. We went
by train to Romsey and trailed back by Stockbridge, seeing much of the Test.

MAY 27 (FRIDAY).

E. We came a week ago: it is now hawthorn time and the hawthorn flower is
very good. This is to be remembered as the great blossom year: we have just
been to see the chestnuts in flower in the tame park and they are very fine. The
tulips in our garden are just over; we have chosen very good kinds and admired
them very much; the iris in the chalk pit has been a wonder. To-day we see the
first flowers of yellow iris by the river. The weather has not been kind: we had
to light the stove again; now it is warmer. To-day there has been great rain, but
it has been warm and still: I would rather have it so than have cold and wind

Hen Blackcap

without the rain. The nightingale is thought to be in the chalk pit, but doesn't speak: there is always one singing in the hedge at night. A Spotted Flycatcher has built in an old thrush's nest of last year by the kitchen window; our tame spink looks to us more than ever for bread and is very tame: it is feeding young in a nest high up in the limes. I found a cock blackcap making the very beginning of a nest in a bramble in the chalk pit. I constantly see him perking about; the hen is much more secret; I have only seen her once. A pair of tree creepers were feeding young in a nest by the Aquarium; a very small nest in a very tight place. The old birds were very unwary, trusting perhaps to the secretness and ungetatableness of the nest.

MAY 30 (MONDAY).
E. Going back to London; we have made much of this month of May, the blossom month in this year of great blossom. Yesterday we trailed over Morn Hill, and Millbarrow down, where we had a cherry luncheon, into and up the valley of the Meon, taking copper beech place in our stride on the way back. The copprets were ready for picking and some were picked. It was a still bright warm day and a great trail. The Sunday before last we trailed to Andover and back and we had one fine evening week-day trail by blushrose mill and Ovington.

JUNE 3 TO 6 (FRIDAY TO MONDAY).
E. Bright days, hot sun, cool N.E. wind, very good early June weather. Much gardening is done now every week; the first tea roses, three Madame Falcots, have just opened. The tulips are over: the iris in the chalk pit still flowers; hawthorn flower is falling and laburnum is the only one of the great blossoms of May which isn't falling or over. We trailed by lady-slipper place, which hasn't a flower yet, and the Alresford green lane. Wrens, treeks*, blue tits and

* Treecreepers.

Mr 'Fishy' Stevenson stands beside his fish shop in West Street, Alresford,
proudly showing off his smart delivery cart

willow wrens and spinks are known to be feeding close to us; the spotted flyke
and blackcap are still sitting: when the cock blackcap isn't heard singing he
may be found sitting on the nest.

JUNE 11 TO 15 (SATURDAY TO WEDNESDAY FOR
ME—TO MONDAY ONLY FOR D).

E. A fine Sunday and a short trail in
which we found a wild open juniper
place in woods high up beyond
Alresford. After Sunday the weather
became wet but not cold: everything
is very soft now and growing fast.
The blackcaps are feeding and the
cock keeps giving out very happy
snatches of song as he flits about in the
limes over the nest. Our garden is
beginning to look established, but is much
worried by moles. We have a good many tea
roses out. Bird songs are ceasing: hardly a blackbird

Mole

now to be heard, no nightingale, only very quiet thrushes and little wisps of warblers' songs.

JUNE 16 TO 20 (THURSDAY TO MONDAY).

E. On Sunday morning the blackcap, which had been singing only very little for some time, burst into the frequent succession of song which we always hear at this time of year. It sounded most happy and seemed to be filling the chalk pit with happiness, but I feared a change in the nest and so it was. All the young had been taken; I suppose by a rook; I heard one cawing and a blackbird fussing at it early this morning. This cast a gloom over our day; but if the blackcap sings*, why shouldn't we? We went a great trail by Medstead village, never scaled before; it is 700 feet high and we found some hawthorn blossom still out and blackbirds singing and put the season back a fortnight. From Medstead we shot down, past gardens and cottages, very strange and new, to near Alton and then trailed steadily to Basingstoke and came back by train to Winchester. One of the young of our tame spink has just eaten bread on the mat and been fed on the step by its mother.

JULY 1.

D. I got here at 12 and found a full summer day. Picked a large bunch of sweet peas and set the room smelling. Then thought that perhaps not enough had been made of the wild forget-me-nots so got a large bowl full and found a rich little clump of musk near where the old willows were cut down. The blackcap is still singing very much in the chalk pit, and the moles are still uprooting the shirley poppy plants there, but the blackcap is more real than the moles. It is sad to see its old nest. Each little stick was put in so softly; I watched it building, and for several hours one day it sang a few notes of happy song just before it put in a stick and just after. There was

Forget-me-nots

* In the chapter titled 'Return of the Warblers' in *The Charm of Birds* Grey writes, 'For perfection or moving quality of voice I should place the blackcap with the blackbird and nightingale in the first-class of British song birds. His song is loud, exceedingly sweet, but also spirited: it is not very long, but it is frequently repeated: there is not great variety, but the thing done is absolutely perfect. There is not a note that fails to please or to be a success. The tone does not stir us so inwardly as that of the blackbird, but it is a sheer delight to listen to it. Of the blackcap, indeed, it has been said that, like the gipsy before the castle gate, "he sang so very completely".'

Hop-picking in the fields near Alton. Most of the hop-pickers came from the East End of London and brought their entire families for this annual event

great happiness in each coming back to the nest, and in each starting away, and in each dive down into the bush. You feel that blackcaps are great nest lovers, and yet this cock was quite happy a few hours after the young birds were taken.

JULY 2 TO 4.

E. We were here last week (Friday to Monday) though we didn't write: it was fine summer weather and we trailed on the Saturday to look at the cottage country near Medstead*: we went slowly about it; going into little shops to find out about the cottages and people and came back by train from Alton. On Sunday we had a sad trail— our ladyslipper was not well out and not very good and the splendid Swarraton musk was all spoiled and eaten by beasts or geese. On our way to Medstead on the Saturday we turned into an old mill near Bishops Sutton; a very snug place, just

* Midway between Itchen Abbas and Alton.

Pink Hawthorn

waiting for someone to make a nest in it. It threw tendrils round us and we talked some talk there that was not quite loyal to Kettidge and had to disentangle ourselves to come away. This Sunday, June 26, was wild rose Sunday. Our Spanish iris were at their best and were picked and taken to London on the 27th.

D. Trailed to Cheriton and saw fine high-standing musk but not quite as much as last year. Then on and lunched near copper beech place and got branches. Then up onto Bramdean common, a fine wild wood, and down to Bishops Sutton where we spent half an hour in the mill house and garden. We saw there some young kinglets, a blackcap and thrushes were singing, two pied wagtails fed a young cuckoo on a rail, and bees were swarming in a window frame. The place was very tangled and sweet looking.

Bullfinch

JULY 21.

D. I have been here since the 14th and stay till the 25th. Every day has been hot, one day only without any breeze. Therm. has not been above 81 under the lime. There is certainly a drought but no bad effects are showing. We water some things in the garden, and roses are coming rather small. The crop of sweet peas is splendid, and mignonette and heliotrope are very good. We have a very tame young blacker and the cross cock comes and the hen occasionally. There are several rather dull young spinks, and even small tail has got rather inclined to snatch the bread and he and spread tail hardly ever came on the mat. It seems to be a bad time of year for tameness in spinks. No sound or sign of the blackcap this time, and no crooning of turtles but many voices of goldfinches and greeners* and sometimes of bullfinches and tittics.

JULY 24 (SUNDAY).

E. Very fine hot days full of sun, but there has been no rain of importance for seven weeks and not enough in July to moisten the surface; and the drought is distressing. Our garden bears up manfully and the plants all show smiling

* Greenfinches.

faces, but they aren't growing and the roses are small. The Ayrshire was magnificent on July 14: I never saw it so splendid: this we think is because we pruned it at the right time last year. I found a linnet with five eggs in the sweet-briar to-day. We started for a trail, but a trailer tyre burst passing the Celt's cottage and we sat under our limes instead and walked the river path walk in the evening. If it had not been for the drought every day in July would have been perfect. Turtles are crooning: we heard a water rail by river path and saw young dabbers, and a dabber* with eggs and a kinglet, and heard a chiffchaff in the glade as we went and a nightjar as we came back, and cottage wren has sung several times. What more could we want except rain?

JULY 31 (SUNDAY)

E. I came on Friday: D. stays on for this week, but this is my last day. The drought is over: there has been good rain; the earth is moist and the weather still warm: we had a fine summer day, with a breeze and white clouds, which didn't interfere with the sun and we trailed to the Juniper place and found it was ragwort and pretty Nancy Sunday. I took leave of everything: I sat in the chalk pit, and had a Chilland evening, and watched the moon up. It was a fine leave-taking evening. I am less sad, because D. is left here and it doesn't seem quite the end. We have seen enormous flocks of sand martins in the sky these last evenings: the flocking of birds is a great sign that the best season is over. We have to be patient now, till we can begin to look forward to the next cottage time.

AUGUST 4.

D. I go to-morrow. The day began by getting to 79 under the limes by 11 o'clock, then came a nice thunder storm and half an inch of rain and

Water Rail

* Dabchick.

Robin

a clear beautiful evening. This morning a willow wren sang quietly about twenty times, and a chiffchaff spoke often during the day in the chalk pit. Small-tail came for bread and the thrush and the old blacker cock, and our dear young blacker eats out of the plate on the rug. I went up to Itchen wood last night and saw a low sun on much ripe corn. The nearest fields are cut. Traveller on all the hedges is good, and some splendid bits had run up a haystack and were flowering. Dear country and dear time.

OCTOBER 23.

D. I came yesterday, a very warm day. Therm. 58 at 6 o'clock and never went below 50 in the night. The Limes are nearly bare but all beeches seem to have all their leaves and are splendid and brown. I picked a rose table full. The chrysanthemums are good, and there is still mignonette. Shirley poppies are out in chalk pit. I have sat out all day, drinking in great peace, and loving my cottage. The bread birds are very wild but I have seen two pair of spinks and a blacker cock, and a robin come to eat. I walked down Chilland meadow towards a splendid sunset, and walked back facing a full moon and a very good star. Foinaven and Arkle* are very fine, but this place is dearest.

NOVEMBER 2.

E. We are having very soft warm days: therm. about 50 and no wind and not always much light. The year seems asleep and the last beech leaves have hung on for a week. There are a good many thin bright brown beeches in tame park; the oaks are thick and very rusty; some elms are green. Nothing moves much, neither the air, nor the clouds, nor the therm. nor the barograph. The autumn has been so dry that it has made it now a dry year: we are glad of this for gardening and planting, but we know very well that we ought to have rain and shall be sorry for our river next year. We are planting bulbs of orris and tulips in the garden which is very easy work; and have made a poppy bed in the chalk pit, which took a very solid day of digging, picking and wheeling: you can do

* Two mountains on the Reay Forest estate in Sutherland, owned by the Grosvenor family, that were to give their names to famous racehorses.

Avington schoolchildren coming home for their midday meal pass the house of three
ladies who did sewing for the local gentry

nothing in a chalk pit unless you take a whole day to it and
work very steadily with heavy tools.

We have only one tame hen spink and a cock,
which looks like small-tail, but is not so tame. A cirl
began to sing to-day, and a valiant wren sings every
morning at sunrise: a thrush practises faintly now
and then but gives up.

NOVEMBER 7.

D. The first rain since I came is falling, and
the rain-gauge seems surprised. A large
rambler-hole in the chalk pit is sucking it in,
and newly planted syringas will be the better
of it. Therm. has been 55 to-day and stove is
hardly necessary. The birds are better: a
thrush is very good, and there are now two
hen blackers, probably mother and daughter. It
is hardly possible to walk once round the cottage
without hearing tittics.

Hen Blackbird

153

NOVEMBER 23.

D. 8 degrees of frost. I went down to Chilland before the sun had melted the white on grass and reeds. Ice was at the edges of side streams, and a slight mist came where it was melting. There was brilliant sun and a light blue haze down the valley and colours were very wonderful. We have had fine and very warm weather since we came, till the glass fell on the 21st and there was an evening of wind and rain. Then it became fine but frosty and cold. Great sadness seems to have fallen over all this Itchen country since Lord Northbrook* died last week. Nothing will ever be quite the same as it was. He was the reason of our having come here, and his kindness made a shelter for us.

Stock Dove

NOVEMBER 29.

D. There have been 14° of frost while I was away. It thawed last night and today but is very cold. It is my last day here, and I planted a prunus triloba by the chalk pit gate, and pulled up shirly poppy plants off the bulb beds. There was a rose coloured sunset which coloured the river. I sat on jaw-hatches to watch it and thought of our coming back here next May with the winter behind us.

* Grey's cousin and the owner of Avington Park across the water-meadows.

1905

WOODMILL

IN THE 1880S THIS WAS THE HEADQUARTERS OF THE
ITCHEN SALMON FISHERY. THE LARGEST SALMON CAUGHT
HERE WEIGHED THIRTY-ONE POUNDS

MARCH 4.

E. We are here for three hours on our way past and have pruned our roses. It is a dull chill day, but birds are singing and spread-tail has appeared again and eaten: he was not here in November. The poor river is in distress: a winter drought has followed the autumn drought and I don't know what will become of our river. There is a plague of voles; they have destroyed our grass and our pinks, for which I grieve, but Susan and all the main things (except the river) are safe and well. There are lots of catkins, but otherwise all looks bare and wintry; you can find the beginnings of tulips and spring things, if you look for them: the spring creeps about the ground secretly.

MAY 2.

D. I came on April 28 from Cassley and the grass everywhere seems very thick and soft after the little wirey Scotch stuff. The wind was blowing cuckoo notes from tame park, and a chiffchaff spoke in a quietly settled way in the chalk pit. I had rather too much gardening to do for the first two days, but the forget me not row is so good and blue and fat that it makes gardening seem worth while. There are no garden sadnesses except that voles have eaten up the east lot of Delphiniums; they are so completely gone that at first I didn't even notice there weren't any. A brood of thrushes and of blackers come to the bread and spread-tail turned up just as I was getting afraid he wouldn't. His tail is quite wonderful. Small-tail comes too, and a pair of old robins feed each other in a foolish sentimental manner standing on the bread. There is a "shooting" blacker nest, and a sitting thrush on cottage, and two broods have already left two other nests. A dunnock is sitting in thuja hedge.

MAY 5 TO 8 (FRIDAY TO MONDAY).

E. Very bright warm beautiful May days and almost beech Sunday: we went

Catkins by the beeches to Wherwell and Longparish and back by the beeches and heard our first wood wren and some other summer birds. I began my nesting by finding a goldfinch building in the chalk pit and a linnet with an egg in Thuja hedge. There is a blackbird with six eggs on Kettidge. Limes not green at all yet.

Hay-making at Manor Farm, Morestead

MAY 12 TO 15 (FRIDAY TO MONDAY).

E. Cloudy and cool till Monday. We trailed to Charlwood
and found the best beech place of all and this was beech
Sunday in it. We lay in an open space in the wood and saw
more beech leaves and better holes of beech trunks and
higher beeches than ever before. Then we went by East
Tisted to Farringdon and saw the mad red building* there,
very mad and costly and unfinished; we came back by a
new way up through a wood with beech undergrowth
and along a high ridge on to the very crest of the Alton
road opposite to Medstead station and so rushed down to
Ropley and then came steadily home. We visited our old mill and
found it still waiting for somebody.

All our nests are unhurt, which is wonderful. Chalk pit Iris is
coming out. Limes are green.

Beech leaves

* Known today as 'Massey's folly'. An unusual red brick building with three towers built by the
Revd Massey for an intended bride. Massey was the vicar of Farringdon for sixty years and started
construction in 1880. It was not completed until 1913, by which time his fiancée had long since
lost interest. He left the house to the Church for educational purposes. It subsequently became a
school and is now owned by T.T. Andreae.

MAY 15.

D. Did not go till 4.50 and saw the sweet peas sticked, and the mignonette and heliotrope bedded out. A sunny day, but not warm. Lime leaves make just enough shade to sit under. The tame spink nests ought to be found, and a feeding robin ought to be followed to its young, but it seems nicer to have the chalk pit quite quiet for the nighter. It is the first time we have ever had one really settled in there.

MAY 19 TO 22 (FRIDAY TO MONDAY).

E. Parching cold winds and drought and not always sun. Sunday was cold, not quite 50 all day, but we went a fine trail to Stockbridge and down the Test to Romsey, stopping at Houghton and Kimbridge and other Test places: the bitter wind helped us all the way. Our nests are still all right, but the birds sit on their young a great deal in the cold. I had a false alarm as to there being a cirl sitting in the sweet-briar, but it turned out a linnet. We heard odd noises at sunset by the high dingles in front of Itchen wood and thought it might be quails*. This has been laburnum, lilac, hawthorn, horse chestnut and broom Sunday and in the chalk pit orris Sunday.

MAY 28.

D. A warm time at last, but not hot. The nightingale moon of last week all wasted by clouds and wind, and could not be sat out under. The bird in chalk pit hardly speaks. The bird in north hedge is better. A red-backed shrike has come to chalk pit, and two pairs of bullfinches most beautifully eat the seeds in the forget-me-not row after we had done breakfast. We trailed to the copper beech place, passing many wretched oak trees and ashes made black by the frost of last Monday. The copper beeches though not seriously hurt were too shrivelled to pick and we came empty away. Our young heliotropes and sweet geranium, and the ivy shoots are all black, but no trees round this place are hurt, and we are grateful for the escape.

Sweet Peas

* Europe's only migratory game bird. Very rare in Britain with occasional 'invasions' from the Continent. They have a preference for calcareous soils.

MAY 26 TO 29 (FRIDAY TO MONDAY).
E. Sudden summer after frost; drought still: birds very anxious for bread, a feeding thrush has become tame.

JUNE 14 TO 20.
D. Came here again after a sad funeral time at Bellshill*. Glad to be quiet and pick up the threads of summer. There has been much rain while we were away, and some this time, and the green is very deep.

    Quantities of birds come for bread, young thrushes fed themselves, four cock spinks come, one eats bread on the mat while E. stands a few inches off. Voles are making themselves beds of the flowers of white pinks and are being caught in jam pots half full of water. One thrush nest over the kitchen door is the only cottage nest. Two Madame Charles roses are all that have come out yet.

Iris

E. We came back after our sad time, very glad to rest and be quiet here. It is a different season now: kind steady summer instead of changeful spring. This has been wild rose Sunday, and oriental poppy Sunday in the chalk pit. We have hardly any tea roses yet: the plants are growing better, but the flowering is bad. The rêve d'ors are in great bloom. We went one evening trail to the top of Morn Hill and heard stone curlews, very far off like ghost cries in the dusk.

JUNE 23 TO 26.
E. Very fine warm summer days and musk time. It is a musk year: the Swarraton musk is better; the watercress man's musk at Alresford is splendid; there are more bits of musk up and down our river than can be counted. English Iris is just out; Spanish is over. We have lots of flowers and the sweet-briar and suckils are out. Birds songs are very few. We went a musk trail and a lady slipper trail and a Medstead Cottages trail and found a very fine green lane to come back by from Medstead. The lady slipper is not good, but the richness of summer and the flowers and scents altogether are more than can be taken in and we are filled.

---

* A little village a few miles to the north of Fallodon where Edward Grey's mother lived. Dorothy and Edward had just returned from her funeral.

Taking sheep to the water-meadows for early spring grass

JUNE 30 TO JULY 3.

E. No trail this time, but a wild park walk one evening and the longest walk since nine years ago on Sunday evening, to the top of Itchen wood and along curious large double hedges to the linnet down water wheel and back by a new bit of green lane and the oat path. We have rather missed the middle distances *Linnet* in these trailing years; we know our garden and chalk pit and meadows very well, and we know distant places. The nests on Kettidge and in the garden have done very well this season: a dunnock fledged for the second time in the Thuja hedge yesterday; we have a linnet feeding young and a flyke on eggs, making a second effort in the same nest: it tried there before but when D. saw it she ordered a soft water tank to be put up close to it and then made extra-natural efforts to save the eggs which lasted for hours but failed. We have a thrush also feeding over the door. The chalk pit nests and the hedge nests have done badly. Our flowers are very pleasant: it is still sweet-briar time: but we have had no big blow of roses and they are coming only gradually and not fine.

JULY 3.

D. A fine hot staying down Monday. E. went early. A honeysuckle and rose breeze instead of the elder flower breeze of last week. Much bird breading has to be done, the two young spinks eat all day long. One which has visible fleas on it is most touching and tame, but it is thought to be going to die. I went down to the bottom of the fishing with a vague feeling in my mind that I had heard an unknown bird sound on Saturday. I sat on the hatches by the great poplar, and wandered, and as I stood on Martyr Worthy bridge I heard it. A most strange sound which I had only half been conscious of before. It was watery and bell-like, six repeated notes with a slightly falling cadence. It had a slight connection with a female cuckoo noise but was certainly not that. It was behind me and I could not judge the distance well, and it was only made once in the hour I was there. It is just possible it was made by an indiarubber toy, or by some sort of foreign bird in the corner Easton cottage, but I think it was in the reeds not far off me. Could it possibly be a bittern*?

This poor cottage has now got a good arm chair instead of the old hard basket one—and a very springy and lovely sofa—the old couch being used for outside sitting. There is also a new blue dado, and new matting on the floor and we have chintz curtains and covers of a blue knotted ribbon pattern on a white ground. I am not sure that all this is right, but I am liking it very much. Brilliant salmon-coloured gladioluses are just coming out.

Bittern

JULY 7 TO 10.

E. Very rich fine summer days; hot. Lime flower is out and we have a tea rose table. We trailed on Sunday to Morn Hill and walked into the warren on the top and lay in the dusk listening to stone curlews: they have a melancholy cry as if they knew they belonged to an age that is gone and were the last of their race. We

---

* It seems unlikely to have been a bittern. Drainage and persecution drove the bittern to extinction as a breeding bird in Britain by 1900, but following recolonization early in the century, a breeding population slowly built up again. There are probably around twenty breeding pairs in Britain today, although bitterns are more widespread in winter when Continental birds arrive.

heard a nightjar* too out on the downs. D. had another surprise in Chilland meadow. I found young whinchats there. There are more young spinks about the bread than we can keep up with: they are now called ruddlers.

Nightjar

JULY 14.

D. I have had seven whole hot days under the limes, smelling them all the time and being glad of them. Long walks and wanders have been done after dinner, and much sitting out with the moon. There has been no rain for a long time but the dryness is not oppressive and the garden is very good. A young cuckoo has been flying about making a noise like a kingfisher. The hen shrike has been much on the north fence of the chalk pit, evidently guarding young, and twisting her tail round and round in an odd way, but I saw no young and no cock. A lovely glow worm was found on Morn hill. It is sad that we so seldom see them. The large side hatch above jaw hatches is being mended at last and much chalk is leaving our chalk pit.

JULY 17.

E. Such nice gentle summer weather, too dry but perfect otherwise. We had a full moon late evening trail by Cheriton musk and Hockly House and Gander down and back by Blushrose mill. Larks and a loud wren and a night sedge are all that sing: the cirl too is heard ringing about. Lime flower has been splendid.

JULY 23 (SUNDAY).

E. Hardly a time at all; I didn't get till midday Sunday and then after a night journey and with a speech on hand. It's horrid to have so short an end and we are clinging desperately to our Kettidge and crying. Lime flower is over and there is nothing special to stay for except the great specialness of Kettidge, and I mind partly because so much of the summer is gone; leaving this marks the end of the best part; but I want Kettidge time never to end; I want it so much that I make believe all the summer that it never will end. Our garden has been

---

* In the chapter titled 'Joy Flights and Joy Sounds' in *The Charm of Birds* Grey writes of the nightjar's song, 'It is of that class of stationary, soothing, continuous sounds, such as the hum of a threshing machine, or the noise of waves on the shore heard at a distance, which dispose us to sit still and listen indefinitely.'

very good in spite of voles; a rich garden compared to what it used to be, and the chalk pit has done well: there has been a brood of shrikes in it. I saw them to-day. Songs are over and the birds not very hungry for bread and the Ayrshire and Suckil and many things are over, but it is all warm and green.

October 19.

D. I came yesterday and Susan says the garden was all good till the night before, when there was much frost. Even chrysanthers are killed, and great fat roses are hanging limp and brown. The leaves of the tall new lilies are like dark jelly. The wallnut tree is hung with black corpse leaves, most unnatural, and the lawn is covered with shrivelled green lime leaves; of course there are also brown lime leaves coming down, but no lovely cream-coloured carpet. The south side of the Avington end of the big lime avenue is quite thick with leaves, but they are the colour of brown beech leaves and look most strange. Oaks still quite green, some elms natural green, and some shrivelled green. The whole country seems quite colourless and odd.

November 20.

E. It is not known why our book has been so much neglected. I haven't had many days here, only week ends, but there have been a lot of these and D. has been here continually. Perhaps we are too well and strong to be properly grateful. The weather has been of all sorts and therefore good. The colour of beeches was destroyed by frost in October, but elms and oaks, especially the big elm road that crosses the big lime avenue have coloured well and the reeds are brown and feathery. Mice have worked horrors in the garden and there are rats, which we almost like for not being mice and being as we hope against mice. Our own spinks are away, but our own thrush and dunnocks come to bread, and so do starlings, which we hope are the ones reared every year in the poplar hole. Our own lime avenue has had a yaffle* every day.

Green Woodpecker

* The green woodpecker.

NOVEMBER 22.

D. The gardening has been delayed by frost and hard ground, but my last evening is very warm with a south changed wind, and I may just get done what has to be done to-morrow morning. A Paul's single crimson rose is to climb up a stick in the chalk pit, and a spring flowering shrub bed has been made and filled. Two new orris beds are made, one with white Florentines and one with Pallidas in, and an oldest of all Celine Forestier rose is put in the bed where Ramblers chose to die. Much Spanish and English orris and some small Pumilas have come into the garden, and the non flowering monbretias have been banished to Relugas, with the non-smelling Duke of Edinburgh roses.

Scarlet Roses
It is thought best to confess that two lots of Danysz virus have been put down to destroy the voles. The destruction of the chalk pit lilacs drove us to this cruelty.

DOROTHY GREY
A Tribute

BY ELIZABETH ROBINS

WINCHESTER CATHEDRAL
WITH ITS DISTINCTIVE BLUNT NORMAN TOWER.
EDWARD GREY WAS AT SCHOOL AT WINCHESTER COLLEGE
FROM 1876 TO 1880

On February 1 1906, just a few weeks after Sir Edward had been appointed Foreign Secretary, Dorothy Grey was thrown from her dogcart while at Fallodon and never regained consciousness. She was only forty-one years old and in the prime of her life.

This delightful tribute by Elizabeth Robins fell from my copy of a privately printed book, *Dorothy Grey* by Louise Creighton, and given to me in April 1999 by Lady Alethea Eliot, Grey's god-daughter. Elizabeth Robins, actress and author, became an intimate friend of Dorothy's and was one of the favoured few invited to stay at the cottage.

Lady Alethea Eliot is the daughter of Sydney Buxton and kindly granted her permission for me to use her father's charming tribute to Sir Edward, which was written after Grey's death in 1933. Lord Buxton was Grey's best friend. Not only were they ministerial colleagues for many years, but they shared the same leisure interests, particularly country pursuits such as fishing. He was Liberal MP for Poplar and became a junior minister, Under-Secretary of State for the Colonies, at the same time as Grey was appointed Under-Secretary at the Foreign Office. Buxton was promoted to Postmaster-General in 1905 and President of the Board of Trade in 1910. He was Governor-General of South Africa from 1914 to 1920 and received an earldom on his return home. He died shortly after his great friend in 1934.

DOROTHY GREY BY ELIZABETH ROBINS

We made acquaintance through the Theatre, an institution in which she took not the smallest interest, and we came to know each other better over the Ibsen plays, which she liked only moderately. Yet when she talked of these matters she said things more real than one often heard from people supposed to know most about them. In spite of her giving one, as the dominant note of her character, an uncompromising 'directness', I think she must have given all those who came close to her a new sensitiveness to the beauty of life. Her power to work this miracle came in part, I think, out of her nearness to what's called Nature. Simple and familiar things easily yielded up for her their essential poetry. Yet I could imagine her

Snowdrops

ready to blame me for saying as much, so
insistently did she strike the note of the plain-
spoken, even the wilfully prosaic. The Hampshire
cottage, all but its pleasant red roof smothered in
creepers 'a green thought in a green shade', she, loving
it as she did, would insist on calling 'the tin house'.
From the little horse she used to drive at Fallodon with
such enjoyment and referred to as 'the insectivorous pony'
up to her favourite poet, she seemed under some
obligation to decline to name any good things in
terms of conventional approval. I never knew a
woman to care so much about the country who
patronized it so little, but the meaning in it and the joy
of it, passed readily from her calm deep realization into
the consciousness of her comrade. Others besides me must

Crab Apple blossom

have felt that existence was a better thing in her presence. That was her
great gift to her friends. She, however, used to say that for her, one of the tests
of character was how a person bore being quite alone. There was something
doubtful if not positively amiss according to her, in any one who shrank from
solitude. I wish I could remember exactly what she said to me once about her
experience of being by herself in some remote place in the West Indies, and
her later recommendation to me of a certain haunt nearer home, where should
I go to live, my chief task (and one she doubted my capacity for) would be to
keep people from following after. And how she reprobated my indifference to
success in that emprise! Her love of quiet country places rather than of people
was certainly an essential part of a nature that shrank from many of the
manifestations of modern social life. She could be scathing enough on the
subject of the deteriorating effect of the town. 'London makes me black inside
and out, but specially inside.' And with this, she had a curiously telling gift
of human sympathy as well as something very like a genius for friendship. No
one could make you feel more surely the glow and strength that came of
nearness to an understanding heart. She had the touchstone quality. Such
people have no need to say much (though I have heard amazed and amused
that she did not talk!), such people have only to be what they are to afford a
test by which life may be tried. Yet she had surprises for you. You might
think you knew where she would be about a given question and behold, she
was quite otherwise, yet with such good reason and such decision that you
saw how inevitably her particular outlook had given her the unexpected view.

She had the faculty of saying quite casually a little sentence that would stick to you for years. I have two or three such laid to her account and I find they have been determining factors in life. For a woman commonly reticent, she could be frank with the frankness of the angels, a frankness that took the breath. There are matters that I have never discussed so intimately with any other creature, and yet after the first amazement to see where we were going, I have felt a dignity in her open dealing that made reserve look mean.

And now that I have set this down, no one realizes better than I that it is a poor dim reflection of her beautiful and haunting presence. I have not even the excuse that she is gone. For, strangely, that is not so for me. When, with a letter to her half-written, I learned in Florida of her death, it seemed to me in the wrench and pain of the moment that I realized, accepted it. But it was not so. Each morning for long after, the thing would come crashing upon me 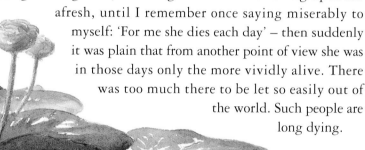 afresh, until I remember once saying miserably to myself: 'For me she dies each day' – then suddenly it was plain that from another point of view she was in those days only the more vividly alive. There was too much there to be let so easily out of the world. Such people are long dying.

Yellow Water Lilies

EDWARD GREY
Bird Lover and Fisherman

BY SYDNEY BUXTON

Pied Wagtail

PRIVATELY PRINTED 1933

For nearly fifty years I enjoyed the privilege of Edward Grey's constant friendship, and was associated with him in politics and in Office on the one hand, and in sport and country life on the other.

Of a truth he had two distinct personalities. If his choice had been free and unfettered, he would have been, and remained, a country gentleman, a life which would for him have been without alloy. But being a Grey, with tradition and example behind him, he was early caught in the toils of politics. When only twenty-three he fought, and rather unexpectedly won, a Northumberland seat, and this he held until he accepted a peerage in 1916.

Naturally, much of Grey's public life, especially when at the Foreign Office, was to him of deep and absorbing interest, and what he did, he did it with his might. But in other ways he felt it to be irksome and burdensome, and what was worse, public duties ever increasingly impinged upon the opportunities of happiness elsewhere. In earlier days, indeed, before real responsibility came, he would, half in jest, half-seriously, express a hope that Providence would be kind and lose him his seat, when he could retire from public life without reproach. There was no affectation in this attitude to life: it went down to the roots of his being. Literally he would much rather catch a 3-lb trout on the dry fly than make a highly successful speech in the House; a quiet morning with his ducks at Fallodon was to him of more moment than some exciting Party success. But his sense of public duty was high, and however great the temptation that might assail him, he took care that it should not be the public weal that would suffer. His character, personality, uprightness, his clear thinking and courage gained for him the confidence of the Country in a very remarkable degree.

But above all, Edward Grey possessed the sense of country and all that it implied. He was

> *A lover of the meadows and the woods*
> *And mountains: and of all that we behold*
> *From the green earth; of all the mighty world*
> *Of eye, and ear.*

This passion did much to keep his brain clear and his mind unclogged.

He had an exceptional knowledge of birds and their ways. Field-glasses in hand, he watched, observed and noted their habits or identified their familiar notes and songs. A walk through the garden and woods of Fallodon with Edward Grey revealed his love for his garden and his exceptional knowledge of, and intimacy with, his shrubs and trees, as though each had for him a separate character and personality of its own; so much so, that when his sight failed he was still able to remember the place, identity and individuality of each one.

Robins and squirrels played a prominent part in Fallodon life. When his approach was observed as he walked down the garden and along the path bordering the pond, the nearest robin would come out of the bushes to greet its friend, and personally conduct him, hopping along the path, or sometimes perched on hand or cap, to the confines of its own territory. It then took its leave and the neighbouring robin took over. Red squirrels were constantly to be seen leaping in and out of the library window, or pattering over the table where Grey was writing, seeking the nuts put ready for their benefit.

Red Squirrel

He was a prominent figure in advocating the protection of wild birds and the creation of bird sanctuaries. Only this year he made one of his rare appearances in the House of Lords in order to support a Bill which dealt with the prohibition of the caging of British wild birds.

As a sportsman Edward Grey did not, I think, care about hunting; and though he greatly enjoyed shooting, especially grouse driving or walking up his partridges at Fallodon, he classed it as a sport far below fly fishing. He was born a fisherman; and as a fisherman, especially as a dry-fly fisherman, he was supreme. He learned to fish and to catch trout on the dry-fly while yet a boy at Winchester. Later, he was one of a few friends who, associated together, took two or three miles of fishing on the Itchen.

There Grey ever waved the wand of the magician. If others of us caught a few fish, he caught many; if we had a blank day (no uncommon occurrence with those subtle trout) he would get a brace. It was always a delight to watch him casting. Fisherman, rod, line, cast, and fly were all in unison. Without apparent effort, the line went out as straight as an arrow, as light as thistledown, or the drag would be overcome by the exact amount of slack – it all looked so simple and so easy. He fished with a stiffish rod, the better to control the hooked fish in a stream abounding in weed beds. Indeed, to me he seemed to be rather hard on his fish – but he landed them. He confined himself mainly to four flies plus the Mayfly. He abhorred oil on the fly and grease on the line as effeminate and messy. Curiously enough he could not fish with his left hand, but made up for the deficiency by greater dexterity with the right. But are not all these and much more written in the book, *Fly Fishing?*

The happiest days of his life were passed at his cottage at Itchen Abbas – a little four-roomed, red-roofed house with a tiny garden behind. Hidden from the road, it lay on a slope within fifty yards from the Itchen flowing between its green and flower-decked water-meadows. On one side of the cottage lay a bird-frequented thicket, and a disused chalk quarry where a pair of kingfishers annually reared their brood.

To him it was a sheer delight to leave Waterloo Station just before six o'clock on a Saturday morning (the House in those days sat on Friday night) and to arrive at the cottage before breakfast on a bright, still June day, with a full day's fishing before him. The noise, the grime, the exhausted atmosphere of London, the distractions and the controversies of House and Office had been left behind, and he was able to breathe in the revivifying and cleansing atmosphere of the cottage, and of the river with its silence and its sounds. These were blissful days for Edward Grey and for his wife, a perfect companion. But heavy sorrow and unlooked-for calamities mysteriously dogged his footsteps. And, gradually, after the War, his eyesight, once so keen, began to fail, due to the pressure and anxiety of his war work, and his vision became more and more obscured; a tragedy indeed to one whose highest pleasures were dependent on his eyesight.

His beloved dry-fly fishing was the first to suffer. The trout, observed and approached, poised near the surface and fully visible in the clear stream, the dimple of a rise, the correct cast, the fly floated within an inch or so of the

Leaping Salmon

spot, the rise, the turn of the wrist –
these comprise the excitement, the
anxiety, the fascination of dry-fly
fishing. But as eyesight began to
fail, so did these fade away; dry-fly
fishing had to be abandoned, and the
Itchen knew him no more.

Salmon fly

Salmon fishing was to him a very great delight,
though not perhaps such an acute pleasure as his dry-fly fishing, inasmuch as
it did not bring into force to the same degree the personal action and skill of
the other. I think that the days of salmon fishing which were to him the most
enjoyable were those passed in the companionship of his brother Charlie,
when he was home between his trips to Africa. That pleasure was doubled if
his brother, handicapped as he was by the loss of an arm, caught more fish in
the week than he did himself. And Grey, indeed, was a wholly unselfish
fisherman, and always delighted in the success of a fellow-angler.

His favourite rivers were the Helmsdale – fished with his great friend,
the late Vernon Watney – the Spey, the Findhorn, and the Cassley. In spite of
increasing blindness, he continued to fish for salmon up to last year, but with
diminishing satisfaction. When no longer able to see where to cast, and when
line and fly were no longer visible, he became more and more dependent on
his ghillie for direction and correction; while playing the fish lost its charm. I
remember his saying to me that one of the thrills in playing a salmon, now
obliterated, was the sudden sight of the scattering spray that marked the line
as it cut the surface of the water when tautened by the hooked fish, or in a
subsequent rush.

Edward Grey's duck sanctuary at Fallodon in Northumberland is well
known by repute, and has been fully described in his *Fallodon Papers*. The
ducks were an absorbing interest in his life and, up to the last, gave him
pleasure and occupation, and it was wonderful how, in spite of his blindness,
he was able to distinguish duck from duck. His understanding of ducks, the
patience displayed in winning their confidence until, as he himself said, 'the
frost of suspicion and fear began to thaw,' was phenomenal.

The Sanctuary consists of two ponds connected by a sluice, the larger of
the two being somewhat less than an acre, together with two or three acres of
rough ground, trees and shrubs, the whole of which, including the garden
adjoining, is surrounded by a fox-proof fence. In this secluded and quiet area
lived a great variety of ducks, some common, others rare. Among these were

tufted duck, pochard, red-headed pochard, shoveller, wigeon, pin-tail and teal, and an elderly eider duck who required special food. Besides these were Mandarin and Carolina wood-duck, Bahama and Chilian pin-tail, Chiloe wigeon, Chilian, ring-necked, and Brazilian teal, and, finally, the canvas-back. Then occasionally, various kinds of wild duck, attracted by the presence of the resident birds, and assured by their demeanour that the place was one of security and calm, paid fleeting visits to the pond, or stayed for a while as guests.

He was successful in rearing no less than five-and-twenty species of duck, some of them very rare, and others which had not been bred elsewhere in England, or at all events under semi-wild conditions. His latest success was the rearing of broods of the American canvas-back. Amongst such a mixed community hybrids were not infrequent, and some of these were of distinguished parentage. These latter he occasionally described as 'High-Bred', a term which, to his amusement, had been used by my typist in a letter of mine, in which I was referring to a rare hybrid that I had reared.

The water-hen, as he called it – known to most of us as the moorhen – is one of the most difficult birds to tame, though they live all their lives cheek by jowl with human beings. He, however, by his patience and by his personality overcame their innate timidity, and latterly, a water-hen was one of the first to come to meet him when he arrived with his basket of bread; while another frequented the lawn and occasionally came into the 'Squirrel Room' in search of food.

In earlier days most of the ducks were pinioned; but for some years past they have been free to fly where they like, and to come and go as they will. Many of them fly away never to return, but a large proportion re-visit their home. Nothing delighted and heartened Edward Grey more than the return of a wanderer, especially if it had been absent for many months and become a wild bird, which yet immediately on arrival took its place in the dinner-queue and again fed from his hand as though it had never been away.

The evening feed – the duck dinner – was sacred, and the convenience of humans went to the wall. The duck is a sunset feeder, and so, of course, the Fallodon ducks must be

Drake mandarin

Edward Grey, Viscount Grey of Fallodon, a few months before he died

fed at that particular time for half-an-hour or so; and, as there was no local Joshua, the house dinner in the summer was varied day by day.

Seated under a great larch tree at the head of the pond he distributed the bread and grain to his ducks crowding round, gobbling up their food, picking at his shoes or plucking at his sleeve to attract attention. He would check the greedy or the forward, encourage the shy or coax the timid bird, and even the wildest fed from his hand. Presently one of them, usually a Mandarin, would perch on his shoulder or on his hat, while others would flap on to the seat beside him.

We will leave him there.

The showers of the spring
Rouse the birds, and they sing;
If the wind do but stir for his proper delight,
Each leaf, that and this, his neighbours will kiss;
Each wave, one and t'other speeds after his brother;
They are happy, for that is their right!

WILLIAM WORDSWORTH